AUTHOR

Alberto Peruffo, was born in Seregno (MI) in 1968, is a history teacher. Graduated from the University of Milan. He cooperated with the Archaeological Superintendency of Milan. He collaborates with several history magazines. He has published the following historical essays: "The Corsairs of the Kaiser" "Marvia editrice", Lombard League 1158 - 1162. The battle of Carcano, "Chillemi edizioni", The triumph of the Lombard League 1174-1176, "Chillemi edizioni", Supremacy of Rome, battles of the Cimbri and the Teutons, "Keltia editrice", Military history of the Ostrogoths, from Teodorico to Totila, "Chillemi edizioni". The Wars of the Peoples of the Sea, "Editions Arbor Sapientiae", The soldiers of the dead head division, The battle of Cortenuova, the battle of Cornate d'Adda, the battle of Capo Colonna and the battle of Desio for Soldiershop series.

A special tanks by the author at Alessandro Botré

Alberto Peruffo, nato a Seregno nel 1968, laureato all'Università degli Studi di Milano. Ha cooperato con la Sovrintendenza archeologica di Milano. Collabora con diverse riviste di storia, insegnante di storia. Ha pubblicato i seguenti saggi storici: "I corsari del Kaiser" "Marvia editrice", Lega Lombarda 1158 – 1162. La battaglia di Carcano, "Chillemi edizioni", Il trionfo della Lega Lombarda 1174-1176, "Chillemi edizioni", La supremazia di Roma, battaglie dei Cimbri e dei Teutoni, "Keltia editrice", Storia militare degli Ostrogoti, da Teodorico a Totila, "Chillemi edizioni". Le guerre dei Popoli del Mare, "Edizioni Arbor Sapientiae", I soldati della divisione testa di morto, La battaglia di Cortenuova, la battaglia di Cornate d'Adda, la battaglia di Capo Colonna e la battaglia di Desio per le collane Soldiershop.

PUBLISHING'S NOTES

None of unpublished images or text of our book may be reproduced in any format without the expressed written permission of Luca Cristini Editore (already Soldiershop.com) when not indicate as marked with license creative commons 3.0 or 4.0. Luca Cristini Editore has made every reasonable effort to locate, contact and acknowledge rights holders and to correctly apply terms and conditions to Content.
Every effort has been made to trace the copyright of all the photographs. If there are unintentional omissions, please contact the publisher in writing at: info@soldiershop.com, who will correct all subsequent editions.
Our trademark: Luca Cristini Editore@, and the names of our series & brand: Soldiershop, Witness to war, Museum book, Bookmoon, Soldiers&Weapons, Battlefield, War in colour, Historical Biographies, Darwin's view, Fabula, Altrastoria, Italia Storica Ebook, Witness To History, Soldiers, Weapons & Uniforms, Storia etc. are herein @ by Luca Cristini Editore.

LICENSES COMMONS

This book may utilize part of material marked with license creative commons 3.0 or 4.0 (CC BY 4.0), (CC BY-ND 4.0), (CC BY-SA 4.0) or (CC0 1.0). We give appropriate attribution credit and indicate if change were made in the acknowledgments field. Our WTW books series utilize only fonts licensed under the SIL Open Font License or other free use license.

For a complete list of Soldiershop titles please contact Luca Cristini Editore on our website: www.soldiershop.com or www.cristinieditore.com
E-mail: info@soldiershop.com

Title: **GERMANIC WAFFEN SS ON THE ITALIAN FRONT. THE "REICHSFÜHRER" AND "KARSTJÄGER" DIVISIONS** Code.: **WTW-009 EN** by Alberto Peruffo. English text translated by Alberto Galli.
ISBN code: 978-88-93275521 first edition February 2020
Language: English Nr. of images: 98 Size: 177,8x254mm Cover & Art Design: Luca S. Cristini

WITNESS TO WAR (SOLDIERSHOP) is a trademark of Luca Cristini Editore, via Orio, 35/4 - 24050 Zanica (BG) ITALY.

WITNESS TO WAR

GERMANIC WAFFEN SS ON THE ITALIAN FRONT. THE "REICHSFÜHRER" AND "KARSTJÄGER" DIVISIONS

PHOTOS & IMAGES FROM WORLD WARTIME ARCHIVES

ALBERTO PERUFFO

BOOKS TO COLLECT

SUMMARY

Introduction .... Pag. 5

THE 16TH SS PANZERGRENADIER DIVISION "REICHSFÜHRER" .... Pag. 7

Himmler's bodyguards .... Pag. 7

The Sturmbrigade "Reichsführer" .... Pag. 9

Corsica operations .... Pag. 10

The formation of the "Reichsführer" division .... Pag. 21

On the bridgehead of Anzio .... Pag. 22

Retired on the Gothic line .... Pag. 24

Anti-guerrilla actions and reprisals on the Apennines .... Pag. 28

Operations on the Senio embankment .... Pag. 29

The last offensive in Hungary .... Pag. 30

Organization charts .... Pag. 33

THE 24° WAFFEN-GEBIRGS-DIVISION DER SS "KARSTJÄGER" .... Pag. 49

Origins .... Pag. 49

Antiband operations on the Karst .... Pag. 53

The formation of the 24th Waffen-Gebirgs-Division SS "Karstjäger" .... Pag. 63

The latest operations .... Pag. 76

Organization charts .... Pag. 79

Conclusions .... Pag. 79

Hierarchy and degrees of SS .... Pag. 81

Bibliography .... Pag. 98

INTRODUCTION

The campaign of Italy, during the Second World War, saw several combat formations of the German army, from the Wehrmacht to the Luftwaffe, among these there were also departments of the Waffen SS or SS fighters who flanked departments of the SS Polizei and intelligence services Germanic.
In the summer of 1943 the Waffen SS in Italy were present only with the Sturmbrigade "Reichsführer", located in the garrison of Corsica, when, with the armistice of September 8, 1943, the Achse plan was activated which envisaged disarming the soldiers Italians in Europe. In Italy the Germans carried out the Alaric operation by implementing the total disintegration of the Italian Royal Army.

Italy was divided by the Germans into two sectors: to the north Erwin Rommel with the Armate B Group and to the south Albert Kesselring, with the rest of the German forces. Hitler had ordered to abandon southern and central Italy considered indefensible after the eventual Italian defection and to join the army of Rommel with his forces. Kesselring rejected this strategic approach, considering, rightly, that the Allies would never have run the risk of landing outside the protection of their aviation, as it actually happened. For this contrast Kesselring resigned on August 14th which Hitler, however, refused. The subsequent exit of Italy from the alliance with Germany on 8 September 1943, and the landing of the Allies in Salerno gave reason to the strategic setting of Kesselring.

In the northern sector was used the 1st Panzer-Division SS Leibstandarte "Adolf Hitler" (LSSAH), present in northern Italy since August 1, 1943, remaining, only, for the short period of disarmament of the Italian armed forces in that area, was soon withdrawn from the Peninsula for other important positions at the beginning of November of the same year.
The "Reichsführer" will be the only unit of the Waffen SS to fight in Italy until, at the beginning of 1944, it will be joined by the 29th SS division "Italien", made up of Italian soldiers assisted by German SS officers, to whom added the 24th division SS "Karstjäger", a mountain unit that will find itself involved in the mountains of Yugoslavia and eastern Italy in the guerrilla war against the partisans.

The 29th SS division will be used mainly in the fight against the partisan guerrillas, with the exception of a battalion involved against the Anzio bridgehead. Among the SS, above all, the soldiers of the "Reichsführer" will stand out, for better or for worse, in the long campaign of Italy. The "Karstjäger" will instead have a great importance in the anti-guerrilla fight against the partisan formations, probably becoming the most experienced German military formation in the partisan struggle. These last two characteristic units of the Waffen SS will be the subject of this research.

▲ Portrait of a Reichsführer man taken during the stay of the assault brigade in Corsica. The uniform is clearly tropical, as the colonial helmet.

THE 16° SS PANZERGRENADIER DIVISION "REICHSFÜHRER"

HIMMLER'S BODYGUARDS

Among the 38 divisions of the Waffen SS formed during the war, the "Reichsführer" division will be the largest SS unit to fight on the southern front, in Italy, for most of its short existence. It was precisely in Italy that the division became infamous for the execution of ruthless reprisals against civilians in the Apennines. In any case, the division distinguished itself in military operations against the Allies fighting, often, in situations of inferiority in the retreat along the Peninsula, from Anzio to the Gothic line, until the last battle alongside the most famous divisions of the Waffen SS in Hungary, merging into the sixth armored army of SS.

The birth of the 16th SS-Panzergrenadier Division "Reichsführer-SS" dates back to the Himmler escort battalion, called Kommandostab RFSS (Reichsführer SS), with functions of personal bodyguard of the SS commander. On May 15, 1941, the formation of the escort was transformed into a battalion called Begleit Bataillon "Reichsführer SS" based at the Oranienburg barracks, a town near Berlin.

This new unit was more than just an SS chief's security escort, having in his staff anti-tank and armored personnel carrier, he surely emulated Hitler's bodyguard whose Leibstandarte SS "Adolf Hitler" had reached the rank of combat formation, already in 1934, as an elite unit of the guard, of regimental dimensions, reaching the force of division, in the early stages of the war, before the invasion of Russia. The Himmler guard department was supposed to become the core of an important military formation like the Leibstandarte and the Luftwaffe division "Hermann Göring", sponsored by the Reich Air Force chief himself.

The battalion was divided into three companies:

1st Kompanie (company)
Motorcyclist platoon
Armored platoon
Anti-tank platoon with Pak pieces of 37 mm

2nd Kompanie
Three motorized rifle platoons

3rd Kompanie
Two anti-aircraft platoons with 20 mm Flak cannons
An anti-aircraft platoon with 37 mm Flak pieces

The battalion was led by SS Sturmbanführer (major) Ernst Schützeck from a long militancy in the Waffen SS of Leibstandarte and Das Reich, whose job was to train the soldiers under his command. Ernst Schützeck, born in 1901, will later have command of SS Panzer Grenadier

Schule in Prosetschnitz, the SS war school in the present Czech Republic, at the end of 1942, maintaining training assignments for various SS units undergoing training until 1944 when he became commander of the SS Panzergrenadier Regiment 38 of the 17th SS Panzergrenadier-Division Götz von Berlichingen, to whose guide he will find death in action on the western front in November 1944.

The majority of the recruits were very young volunteers or volksdeutsche, soldiers of Germanic origin coming from areas outside the original borders of the German Reich, without the constraint in being precepted by the Wehrmacht.
The training was soon terminated when the battalion was transferred in September 1942 to the 50th Teses Army Corps, on the Eastern front in the sector of Leningrad, under the direct dependence of the 2nd SS Infanterie Brigade powered, led by the SS- Brigadeführer Gottfried Klingemann, already in service at the Kommandostab Reichsführer SS until October 1941.
The battalion was immediately involved in hard clashes between 3 and 14 October in Kolpino, a town east of the besieged city of Leningrad, where, the Red Army, was trying to break through the German lines to free the city surrounded by Germans.

At that time, the SS-Sturmbanführer Herbert Garthe was in command of the battalion, who had replaced Schützeck on 20 November.
The battalion participated in the defense of Krasny-Bor, east of Kolpino, where he remained throughout the month of December to fight in an icy landscape dominated by large forests. The 3rd company was temporarily detached to participate in a limited offensive aimed at shortening the front line, towards the town of Tikhvin, more than 150 kilometers east of the rest of the battalion.
On January 7, the Russians, from General Vlasov's second army, launched a major offensive along the frozen Volchow River between Lake Ladoga in the north and Lake Ilmen in the south. The intention of the Soviets was to reach Leningrad and break the siege when the German army, in full, was in serious difficulty on the whole Eastern front, after having withdrawn in front of Moscow. To prevent the breakthrough of the German lines in that sector, defenses were strengthened and the battalion of the "Reichsführer" was transferred between the villages of Mjasny-Bor and Spassakaya-polist along the Volchow, helping to stem the Russian attacks.

The Soviet offensive in front of Moscow had put the Germans in troubles and forced them to the defensive in appalling climatic conditions due to the Arctic frost that had unleashed on their armies. Hitler's will to resist at all costs allowed the front line to hold on despite the fact that there was an important loss of ground in the central sector, in front of Moscow, at the same time as the formation of some pockets in the Leningrad area, the most important was that of Demjansk, in a wooded area in the region south of Lake Ilmen, where the SS Totenkopfdivision division was trapped together with other units.

To counter heavy Russian T 34 tanks, 37mm anti-tank guns will prove largely inadequate. For this reason, the powerful antiaircraft were reinforced, but also anti-tank, 88 mm SS cannons of the SS Flak Abteilung Ost, with the strength of a battalion, with which they could repel the continuous Soviet offensive attempts in that area. In battles the battalion commander, Garthe, was seriously injured on February 3, 1942, and Sturmbannführer Karl Franz Grimme took command in his place after the department had been led for a short time by SS Obersturmführer (lieutenant) Spelter for lack of senior officers.

In the spring of 1942 the Germans managed to break the siege of the bag of Demyansk to go on the counterattack, repelling the Russians across the Volchow River, eastward, on May 7th, a circumstance in which the SS battalion was the protagonist, fighting between swamps and forests in the Volchow River area. The subsequent Russian offensive in August was blocked with the Germans who managed to surround the entire second army of Vlasov in a large nesting bag which led to the total destruction of the Russians in October of that year.

At that time, however, the Himmler battalion was far from the front, having been withdrawn from the front line to be reorganized in Germany as early as June 20. The remains of the battalion returned to being used as the Reichsführer's Kommandostab while, in Russia, only a few soldiers remained who were occasionally employed in counter-guerrilla operations in the German rear in Ukraine, within other departments organized for the needs incumbent in the fight against the partisans between August and November 1942. At that time, the men who joined the SS Reichsführer division, and then participated in the reprisals against civilians in Italy, would experience the fight without quarter against the Russian partisans, in a situation where each civilian was considered an enemy to be mercilessly eliminated and none of the contenders took prisoners or showed mercy.

The soldiers of the SS battalion were grouped again at the beginning of December 1942 in Arys and then moved to France in late February of the following year where the battalion was transformed into Sturmbrigade.

THE STURMBRIGADE "REICHSFÜHRER"

The decision to create the Sturmbrigade was made at the Truppenübungsplatz (training camp) in Debica on February 14, 1943, starting with the motorized battalion. It was then decided to send vehicles and soldiers to France where the new department would mass and train.

Upon arrival in France, in the Rennes training camp, in February 1943, the Sturmbrigade or assault brigade, still had the staff of a battalion of about 800 soldiers. Over time the number of soldiers was implemented with new recruits and new vehicles including Flak's powerful 88mm antiaircraft guns that could also be used in anti-tank function and a battalion of assault wagons Sturmgeschütz StuG III Ausf F with four crewmen. Schematically the staff was the following:

Brigadestab (Brigade Command)
Grenadier-Bataillon (Grenadier Battalion)
Panzerjäger-Abteilung (Tank hunting battalion)
Sturmgeschütz-Abteilung (Assault tank battalion)
Flak-Abteilung (Anti-aircraft battalion)

The Sturmbrigade was commanded by the SS Obersturmbannführer Karl Gesele and was composed of a battalion of grenadiers on 6 companies, a Panzerjäger battalion on 3 companies, a Sturmgeschütz battalion of 3 batteries with StuG III Ausf F tank hunting, each battery had 3 platoons with 3 assault tanks, and finally a Flak battalion that had 4 batteries with 88 pieces and 20 mm Flak cannons. In fact, the latter department operated, already in March 1943, in the Borisov-Minsk area, engaged in the fight against the Russian partisans in the "Kottbus" operation together with the notorious Oskar Dirlewanger1, before being reunited with the rest of the brigade in Italy.

In July of that year, the Sturmbrigade was transferred to Corsica where it was supposed to have garrisoned the coast pending a possible Allied landing. Corsica belonged to the Italian crown as an unredeemed land, torn from France in 1940. In June 1943 the Axis commands wanted to reinforce the garrison of the two large islands of the Tyrrhenian Sea. After the loss of North Africa, it was far from obvious which direction the next Allied offensive would take. Perhaps in Sicily or in the Balkans, as hypothesized by Churchill, but an invasion of Sardinia and Corsica that would have allowed the Allies to directly threaten the Tyrrhenian coast of Italy and, above all, the coast of southern France was not to be excluded. The inability to fully exploit the air cover will decide the Allies to discard an attack on Sardinia, preferring Sicily and, subsequently, a less daring advance along the Apennine ridge, relegating the Sardinian island and Corsica to completely secondary fronts. However, a fortunate disinformation work carried out by the British secret services led the Germans to consider Sardinia and Corsica one of the main objectives of the Allied offensive.

The Mediterranean theater saw, for the first time, the action of SS units in the Mediterranean theater. This is interesting, also from the point of view of uniformology, with the SS of the "Reichsführer" who wore the equipment and the German tropical uniform, something almost unique among the Waffen SS.

Corsica operations

Until the intentions of the enemies were clear, the garrisons of the two Tyrrhenian islands were strengthened with first choice units.
In the summer of 1943, five Italian infantry divisions and the Nembo paratrooper division were stationed between Corsica and Sardinia, to which must be added the Italian coastal divisions, consisting of five divisions and two brigades, however poorly armed departments formed by reservists . The Germans deployed the 90th mechanized division in Sardinia, and in Corsica the Sturmbrigade "Reichsführer".
On this island the Italian garrison departments that flanked the SS were: the Cremona and Friuli infantry divisions, flanked by the 225th and 226th coastlines which, with other smaller departments, were in command of the general of Armata Giovanni Magli, for a total about 80,000 men in Corsica. Between Sardinia and Corsica the Germans deployed about 12,000 men under the command of Generalleutnant Fridolin von Senger und Etterlin and in Corsica in addition to the Sturmbrigade there was an infantry regiment (3 ° / 870) inserted in the ranks of the SS brigade.

▲ At the command of the torpedo boat Aliseo, on 9th of September of 1943, Carlo Fecia di Cossato managed to block the German attempts to land reinforcements at Bastia, at that moment in Italian hands. Carlo Fecia di Cossato was an officer of integrity and faithful to the crown, he was deeply marked by the events of September 8th that pushed him to take his own life. You can see the numerous German decorations of which he was awarded.

During the period prior to September 8 the task of the SS was to supervise the coast of Corsica, leaving the interior in the hands of the French resistance, the "Maqui" who were hiding on the inaccessible mountains of the island waiting for the right opportunity to Get into action. On the evening of September 8, 1943, the Germans found themselves in marked inferiority in that chessboard. Nonetheless von Senger und Etterlin was confident of being able to disarm the Italian departments and retain possession of the two islands, this in consideration of being able to receive reinforcements from the continent through the port of Bastia in northern Corsica.

In fact, the Germans occupied the strategic port of Corsica the same night, forcibly disarming the Italian garrison, totally taken aback by the events. Among other things, the news of the armistice had reached General Magli while he was having dinner with von Senger und Etterlin who ensured that he did not want to harass the troops of the former Italian ally. But Bastia was too important for the Germans not to get hold of it right away.
On day 9, in Corsica, there were sporadic clashes between Italian and German soldiers, arising more from tension than from a precise military decision. However, it was in Bastia that, at the dawn of that day, the Italians of the Friuli division attacked the German contingent of the infantry regiment barricaded in the city. The battle on the streets was short but intense and at 8 am the Corsican town was once again in the hands of the Italians, with the Germans complaining of heavy losses, some sources speak of about 500 fallen.
The decisive clash for the fate of Corsica took place, that same day, in the mirror of the sea in front of the port of Bastia, when the Germans tried to bring reinforcements from the continent. Here the Aliseo torpedo boat under the command of Carlo Fecia di Cossato (valiant commander of submarines and gold medal for valor, as well as decorated with the Ritterkreuz) managed to sink seven German naval units, with superior armament to his own, in a single battle, definitively ending von Senger und Etterlin's hope of keeping Corsica German.
In the very next days, the two sides maintained their positions with the Italians settled in Bastia.

Magli informed of the influx of the 90th mechanized German division through the Strait of Bonifacio, including a thousand Nembo paratroopers, who remained loyal to the alliance with the Germans, decided to go on the offensive. The Italians who were masters of the west coast, including Ajaccio, occupied the important communication routes on the east coast of the island. Magli placed numerous checkpoints along the coastal road leading to Bastia, helped in this action by Corsican partisans, excellent connoisseurs of the terrain.

The Sturmbrigade was located in southern Corsica from 8 September to create a bridgehead to facilitate the landing of German troops from Sardinia, which began already the following day. With the influx of the 90th panzergrenadier division, the Germans advanced north of Corsica along the east coast, with the SS of the Sturmbrigade acting as a tread, destroying the various checkpoints and foiling ambushes along the winding road. At sunset on day 13, the Panzergrenadier of the "Reichsführer" supported by the StuG of the assault battalion attacked Bastia, starting the decisive battle of the campaign. The infantrymen of Friuli defended themselves fiercely, but, despite their numerical superiority, they could not compensate for the armored vehicles of the Sturmbrigade.

In those days the myth of the presence of Tiger tanks was born among the armored vehicles of the SS. So much was the fame of that weapon that every tank or assault vehicle immediately became, for Italian soldiers, a Tiger tank. Such was the persistence of these stories in the memorials that even a certain historiography takes for granted the presence of the Tiger panzers, to whom he attributes the success of the German offensive on Bastia. In reality, between the ranks of the "Reichsführer" there were not even tanks in the strict sense, but only StuG III Ausf F assault vehicles in which, the limited swing of the cannon, in a fixed turret, was a disadvantage in mountainous and hilly terrain like those of Corsica.

The main clash took place in Casamozza, a small village south of Bastia, where the SS managed to open a breach and already on the morning of the 14th they occupied Bastia and its important port. In the clash the Italians had had many fallen and well 2,000 prisoners, many others had found refuge in the rugged mountains of the region, where they will wander for several days in hunger. On the 14th, allied troops began to land in Ajaccio. These were in particular French soldiers under the command of General Martin with whom Magli cooperated. The coordination and the number of French troops in Corsica was however not sufficient to block the German troops and prevent them from re-boarding in Basita.
The clashes continued until early October with the soldiers of the "Reichsführer" committed to guarding the road on the east coast of Corsica and, above all, to defend the port of Bastia, from which German troops now left the island en masse, without that the allied navy, strenuously engaged in Salerno, could do nothing to block maritime traffic. The last fight thus took place around Bastia on 4 October, when French troops were able to enter the city completely destroyed by Allied bombings when it had already been abandoned by German soldiers, who had safely left Livorno the night before.
The casualties during the campaign were 700 German soldiers and 350 prisoners. The Italians were 800 killed, mostly in the Friuli division, while the French had 75 dead 12 missing and 239 injured.

The end of the campaign in Corsica saw all the participants consider themselves in some way winners: the Italians who remained masters of the land had their only victory over the Germans who managed to drive away from the islands of Sardinia and Corsica. The French conquered Corsica, the first French province to be liberated, while the Allies conquered the two strategic islands of the Tyrrhenian Sea without having to divert heavily engaged troops to Salerno and southern Italy.
The Germans for their part could be satisfied with having rescued their troops from a very critical situation that saw them in a clear numerical inferiority and isolated on the sea from the powerful enemy navy that could also count a clear aerial supremacy.
The German army report was able to announce three days after leaving Corsica: "In the fight on the island of Corsica the SS-Sturmbrigade was particularly distinguished". The brigade was withdrawn in Italy with the anti-aircraft battalion deployed in Liguria to defend the ports and the coast from opposing air strikes, unlike other departments that were transferred to Slovenia in the area of the capital Ljubljana. This not before having sent about ten assault wagons and motorized departments of the Sturmbrigade through the streets of Rome in October, the only SS departments to march along the Roman roads in order to impress the local population with a display of power Teutonic.

▲ Assault cannons StuG III Ausf F of the Sturmgeschütz battalion of the Reichsführer retreating northwards along the roads of Corsica (Bundesarchiv Corsica 43)

▲ Wagon StuG III Ausf F of the Reichsführer, you can see the SS characteristics, symbol of the brigade and then of the division. (Bundesarchiv Corsica 43)

▼ Reichsführer's StuG III Ausf F wagons moving along the roads of Corsica. The cloth on the mouth of the cannon could indicate that the photo was taken before 8 September. (Bundesarchiv Corsica 43)

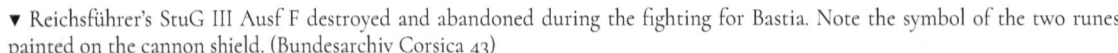

▲ Another picture of the Reichsführer's tank hunting battalion, the tropical uniforms worn by the SS men are clearly visible. (Bundesarchiv Corsica 43)

▼ Reichsführer's StuG III Ausf F destroyed and abandoned during the fighting for Bastia. Note the symbol of the two runes painted on the cannon shield. (Bundesarchiv Corsica 43)

▲ A SS guard soldier in Corsica in typical tropical uniform

▲ Another photo of the Panzerjäger battalion of the Reichsführer marching along the tortuous roads of Corsica. (Bundesarchiv Corsica 43)

▲ The roads of Corsica were ideal for ambushes, while the German tank fighters Sturmgeschütz with their fixed casemate cannon were certainly not ideal for fighting on that type of rough terrain. (Bundesarchiv Corsica 43)

▲ Flak battalion anti-aircraft artillerymen in action with their 88 mm piece, in an unspecified location (perhaps Liguria), during the hot September 1943

▼ Same 88 battery in action. Notice the helmets with the classic SS camouflage sheets.

▲ Group photo of Reichsführer soldiers in one of their camps wearing tropical uniforms.

THE FORMATION OF THE DIVISION "REICHSFÜHRER"

In October 1943 it was decided to expand the armored grenadier division brigade with the contribution of new volksdeutsche volunteers. The division was given the number 16, becoming the 16th SS Panzergrenadierdivision "Reichsführer-SS" (RFSS). Between 23 September and 3 October the new division in formation was located in Livorno where about 7500 recruits gathered. Around October 20, the brigade, which would soon become a division, was deployed to defend the coast between Civitavecchia and Cerveteri. On October 16, 1943, the SS-Gruppenführer Max Simon, coming from the SS-Totenkopf (SSTK) division, was assigned to command the new unit being formed, replacing Gesele who will then be chief of staff of the division from December 944 to January of the following year. Max Simon was the first commander of the 16th SS division who drove for a whole year, throughout the Italian countryside.

The staff included two panzergrenadier regiments, numbered from 33 to 34, shortly after renumbered 35 and 36, following the numerical progression of the other existing SS regiments. In November 1943 the parts of the division began to take place, albeit under staff due to the difficulty of finding men and means, being concentrated in Italy in the Livorno area. In December the division was subjected to LI Gebirgs-Korps of the fourteenth Armee of northern Italy as a reserve unit and had reached the strength of 12,720 men, although it continued to suffer from a shortage of officers and non-commissioned officers, as well as a shortage in equipment.

Several soldiers from other SS units, in particular from Totenkopf, were transferred to the "Reichsführer", together with young recruits of the SS-Panzergrenadier-Lehregiment training regiment. Despite this, in the late spring of 1944, 4500 recruits belonging to the 16th SS Panzergrenadierdivision "Reichsführer" were diverted to the SSTK division, engaged on the eastern front. Ties between SS-Totenkopf and "Reichsführer" were always close with many officers and soldiers being transferred from one unit to another. This close relationship is also evidenced by the fact that all the commanders of the 16th SS division came from Totenkopf. The organization chart of the division was structured as follows:

Kommandeur SS-Divisions-Nachschubtruppen 16 (divisional command battalion and supplies)
SS-Panzergrenadier-Regiment 35 (35th SS armored grenadier regiment)
SS-Panzergrenadier-Regiment 36 (36th SS armored grenadier regiment)
SS-Panzer-Aufklärungs-Abteilung 16 (16th SS reconnaissance battalion)

SS-Panzer-Abteilung 16 (16th SS armored battalion) SS-Sturmgeschütz Abteilung 16 (16th SS tank hunting battalion) SS-Pionier-Abteilung 16 (16th battalion of the SS genius) SS-Artillerie-Regiment 16 (16th SS artillery regiment) SS-Flak-Abteilung 16 (16th Flak SS anti-aircraft battalion) SS-Sanitäts-Abteilung 16 (16th SS health battalion) SS-Feldgendarmerie-Kompanie (SS Military Police Company)

To these were added: SS-Wirtschafts-Bataillon 16 (16th SS battalion) SS-Feldersatz-Bataillon 16 (16th training battalion and SS reserve) SS-Nachrichten-Abteilung 16 (16th SS battalion for transmissions and reports)
At the beginning of 1944 the division was still in the process of organizing and completing the ranks when the Allied landings took place in Anzio, just south of Rome. To deal with this emergency two Kampfgruppe (combat units) were created with the units in efficient division and sent to fight the enemy on the bridgehead.

On the bridgehead of Anzio

The Kampfgruppe named "Dieterich" from the name of its commander the SS-Oberführer (colonel-brigadier) Karl Dieterich, the highest capable officer of the SS in that operating theater, was composed of the 2nd grenadier battalion of the 35th regiment, veteran of the Sturmbrigade. The Kampfgruppe "Knoechlein" was led by SS-Obersturmbannführer (Lieutenant Colonel) Fritz Knoechlein, Totenkopf veteran who, at the end of the conflict, will be hanged by the British for the killing of 80 British soldiers in Le Paradis, which took place during the campaign of France in May 1940. In this case it was the 2nd battalion of the 36th regiment formed, in large part, by recruits to constitute the department. Later, the command of the latter Kampfgruppe will pass to the SS-Hauptsturmführer (captain) Vetter, who will change the name of the unit itself.
To these were added the complete 16th Flak SS antiaircraft battalion, with elements of the exploration department of the SS-Panzer-Aufklärungs-Abteilung 16 who found himself

involved in the fighting southeast of Cisterna in February, together with the departments of the "Reichsführer" a Barbarigo battalion of the X MAS and a battalion of the 29th SS division "Italy" led by SS-Obersturmbannführer Carlo Federigo degli Oddi were assigned to reinforce. The German units left Ljubljana in a hurry with the SS of the Kampfgruppe "Knoechlein" who, without vehicles, had to rely on courier driven by civilians, arriving staggered in southern Lazio after a tiring journey, troubled by air attacks and bad weather . The deployment of this force on the bridgehead took place from January 25 and lasted until April in a defensive position along the localities of Sessano and Isola Bella, in line along the Mussolini canal and the road between Cisterna and Sessano, on the southern side of the Allied bridgehead, about 13 kilometers from the sea. The locations affected by the clashes bore names that referred to the First World War, such as: Borgo Carso, Borgo Flora, Borgo Podgora and Borgo Sabotino, and, just as in the past war, the infantry involved in that area, faced a position war inside of wet and muddy trenches.

The departments of the "Reichsführer" division had their base in the rear in Terracina and assigned to the 715th German Infantry Division (Infanterie-Division), led by General Major Hildebrandt, placed under the command of the German 14th Army. The Kampfgruppe "Knoechlein" positioned itself south of the Mussolini canal with the marines of the Barbarigo battalion, while the men of the 35th SS regiment found their position along the line of the north front of the canal itself. The battalion of the Italian SS will arrive only in mid-March and was distributed between the two Kampfgruppe, taking over the men of Barbarigo.

The sector was relatively quiet, sheltered from the enemy and German offensive routes of February, being considered ideal to familiarize yourself with the harshness of the front of inexperienced departments and never tried, before, in battle. For this reason, under the 715th infantry division, several and heterogeneous units followed, of the Luftwaffe and Italian, even some companies of the ROA (Russian liberation army, composed of former prisoners of the Red Army), of which there was no certain of their moral strength in combat.

At that time the clashes were limited to night patrols that explored no man's land, trying to penetrate the opposing lines to take prisoners or to lay down and eliminate the numerous minefields scattered on flat and uniform terrain. During the day, the soldiers were holed up in their muddy shallow holes because of the sub-surfacing groundwater that prevented digging deeper shelters of half a meter, with camouflaged positions spread in depth, scattered along the defensive territory. The war was the typical one of a position where, during the day, the contenders limited themselves to exchanges of artillery and mortar shots which damaged the defenses; only at night did the actions of small patrols and the reconstitution work of the trenches damaged during the day. The Germans had mixed forces with elite units to counter the terrain, including the 504th Paratrooper Regiment of the 82nd Division and the 4th Battalion of American Rangers, later replaced by the 34th US Infantry Division (Infantry Division).

To make things going from bad to worse for the Germans, there was the total domination of the skies that the Allied planes had now reached, to which were added the shots of the large calibers of the enemy ships that crossed in front of Anzio. The power of the naval artillery shooting was demonstrated when the "Dieterich" platoon of engineers made overnight reproductions of armored vehicles in canvas and wood, called Panzerattrappen, inside a grove just behind the German front line. Already at dawn, the allied observers were able to communicate the position of what they considered an enemy gathering, directing the shot of the large calibres of the battleships and cruisers on the area of the grove which was reduced to ash.

In the night patrol actions the departments of the Italian SS distinguished themselves including the Platoon Arditi, commanded by the future great orientalist, the SS-Untersturmführer (second lieutenant) Pio Filippani-Ronconi, who was seriously injured by the explosion of a mine during a night action on April 14th. In early March the antiaircraft battalion also flowed to Anzio, joining the three SS battalions that fought in that area. In the meanwhile the rest of the "Reichsführer" division was transferred, already in February, to eastern Hungary, in the Debrecen area, where it participated in Operation Margarethe, taken in April 1944, which led to the German military occupation of the Magyar country favoring the taking of power by Admiral Horty. On that occasion the parts of the division, with the staff still largely incomplete, were gathered as Kampfgruppe called "Simon", from the name of its commander, adding elements of the 5th SS-Panzer-Division "Wiking" and the reformed Begleit Bataillon "Reichsführer SS".

In the night between 16 and 17 April all the departments of the 16th SS Panzergrenadierdivision present in Anzio were silenced withdrawn from the fighting line in order to reunite the complete division in the Grosseto area that was going to gather there. On the bridgehead remained the battalion of the 29th SS division while the Kampfgruppe of the "Reichsführer" were replaced that same night by the 1028th Infanterie-Regiment belonging to the 715th division and to which the Italian SS will go.

Retired on the Gothic line

In mid-May, the 16th SS division was reunited in Tuscany between Lucca, Pisa and Grosseto, with the task of garrisoning the coasts in front of the island of Elba and controlling the Aurelia road that led to Rome, a city now close to be conquered by the Americans. The division was under the control of the 75th Army Corps, led by the infantry general (General der Infanterie) Anton Dostler, who controlled the area between Tuscany and Lazio, located on the right wing of the 14th army that had control on the western sector of the Italian front. Subsequently, during the retreat to the Gothic, the "Reichsführer" will be part of the fourteenth armored Corps, led by General von Senger und Etterlin. This armored Corps, in addition to the 16th division of the SS, had among its ranks the 26th armored division, the only department of this type to remain employed in Italy until the end of hostilities, and the 65th infantry division, with, in reserve, the Luftwaffe's 20th field division.

For the first time assembled and fully staffed, the SS grenadiers division, with a strength of 16,976 men, would have had to face the advance of the Allies northward, trying to delay their movements as much as possible to allow time for the German army to strengthen on the Gothic line on the northern Apennines. This was to happen with a division still with few means and with a large part of the staff still in training. On June 3 the division was consolidated by the SS-Panzergrenadier-Lehr-Brigade. At the same time the first clashes took place against the Allies advanced in the Grosseto area, which involved the 16th battalion of the SS genius (SS-Pionier-Abteilung, led by the SS-Sturmbannführer Erwin Lange) and the 16th SS reconnaissance battalion (SS -Panzer-Aufklärungs-Abteilung, led by the SS-Sturmbannführer Walter Reder[1] since December 1943).

On June 27 the command post of the 16th division was overtaken by the advance of the 34th American division (Red Bulls), belonging to the fifth army, at the village of San Vincenzo, just north of Populonia, forcing the Germans to hide behind enemy lines to then return to their lines with dangerous night marches.

The retreat continued as far as Cecina, along the coast, where the division met on a new defensive line at the end of June, created in order to slow down the adversary's advance along the Cecina river for a few days. On this occasion, to support the SS, the Tiger tanks of the 3rd company of the 504th armored battalion of the army arrived (s.Pz.Abt.504), also retreating from Anzio, which helped to block the enemies for a few days. From the northern side of Cecina, the Germans faced the offensive of the 34th American division on 30 June, supported by a violent artillery preparation shot and armored vehicles. Particularly tough clashes occurred between the 2nd battalion of the 135th US infantry regiment and the divisional command company, SS-Division Begleit Kompanie, led by the SS-Hauptsturmführer (captain) Max Paustian, on altitude 35, south of Cecina, which allowed to control the homonymous inhabited area. Here the SS, although in numerical minority, managed to repel the majority of enemy attacks, despite the fact that the attackers managed to build a bridgehead north of Cecina, already on June 29, in the area near the coast.

At dawn of the following day, the Americans launched a new offensive in force, trying to take the position on their side, in order to avoid a direct attack on Altitude 35, in this way the second battalion of the 35th regiment of the SS, under the command of the SS-Sturmbannführer (major) Cantow who defended the left side of Quota 35. The clash took place in the early hours of the morning, finally, the defenders were forced to move back towards the river, recreating a defensive line with the remainder of the division and the departments of the Luftwaffe's 19th field division which were on the left side of the SS.

Also a little further away, the first battalion of the 35th regiment had been forced to withdraw from Altitude 82 on day 30, and then attempt to regain the lost positions with a counterattack in the following morning, managing to re-occupy Altitude 82. Otherwise, the German assaults on the bridgehead north of the Cecina river, could not repel the enemy beyond the river which, from that point, had the possibility of launching raids, deep, along the coast, towards the north, risking to isolate the German departments that fought near the town of Cecina.

On July 2, the Americans entered in a Cecina devastated by fighting, forcing the 3rd battalion of the 35th regiment, of the SS-Obersturmführer (lieutenant) Fritz Horn who defended the coastal area, to retire after fighting valiantly between the houses of the country. All the passages on the river were destroyed by the Germans who retreated north, along a flat plain of sparse woods and bushes that sloped towards the sea environment which made it difficult to organize a defense given the absence of orographic holds, this always pressed by the enemies who advanced rapidly.

At Cecina the SS had fought boldly, taking into account the heterogeneous training and a discipline that was not always impeccable, suffering significant losses which, however, did

---

1 Walter Reder (1915 - 1991) came from the 3rd SS Totenkopf division where, on the eastern front, under the command of the 1st battalion of the 1st SS-Panzergrenadier regiment, on 3rd April 1943, he obtained the coveted decoration of the Knight's Cross following the victorious offensive battle of Jeremejewka on 14th February 1943 in the operations for the reconquest of the Ukrainian city of Kharkov by the 1st SS Panzer korps consisting of three divisions of the SS. Reder will be seriously wounded on 9 March in the suburbs of Kharkov, losing his left forearm.

not affect the morale of the division. The new defensive line of the division was established in Rosignano with difficulties due to the lack of fresh troops to support and shortage of supplies which, often, were missing due to the attacks of the partisans along the communication routes. The fuel shortage forced the Germans to abandon several means of transport on the road to retreat. The Rosignano area had to undergo extensive destruction by the Germans who made scorched earth, in particular the port area of the Rosignano-Solvay was destroyed, while the SS were fortified, camouflaging their positions, along the coastal caves and along the slopes of the hills north of the town which, finally, created a hilly area easy to defend.

On 3 July the American soldiers of the 34th division attacked Rosignano itself, supported by armored vehicles, managing to penetrate the town with the SS engaged in defending themselves in the town throughout the day, launching local counterattacks that were rejected. During that night the Germans were attacked by the Americans, with the partisans who supported the action. Even on the hills west of Rosignano, just south of the town of Castellina Marittima, the Germans of the SS had to resist the American offensive at Quotas 317 and 389, managing, in this case, to repel the attackers.

After a brief pause in the clashes, on July 6, the Americans resumed attacking Rosignano along the coast, after a heavy artillery preparation shot, catching on the flank the Germans who find themselves circumvented by the enemy in the west. Without supplies, especially in ammunition, the defenders had to give ground and retreat north to avoid being surrounded. On the eastern side, west of Castellina, the 2nd battalion of the 36th SS regiment, with the help of some tanks stormed Sturmgeschütz, managed to block the enemy advance with a counterattack that forced the Americans to retreat in that sector, avoiding the Germans to end up surrounded on that side.

The Germans decided to retreat, which happened without too many accidents despite the complete domination of the skies of the Allies who occupied Livorno in mid-July.

The new defensive line stood towards Pisa, where the Arno river would have guaranteed an excellent obstacle to the advance of the fifth enemy army that went up the Tyrrhenian coast. The fulcrum of the Americans' action in that area was Florence, where the allied commanders competed to finish first for a matter of mere prestige, as had happened with the conquest of Rome and, in the same way, the directives of the most profitable advances that would have put the Germans in greater difficulty. Precisely for this reason the "Reichsführer" defended itself north of the Arno and Pisa in an unchallenged way in mid-July, so the SS remained calm in their new positions which were only meant to slow down the enemy advance towards the fortifications of the Gothic in the Apennines.

On July 17 all units of the SS division had passed north of the Arno and the bridges blown up on July 23, making machine-gun nests between the fields and the city buildings on the other side while the soldiers took possession of the buildings of the city. In this way the Normale of Pisa was transformed into a barracks with the command of the town square entrusted to the commander of the 2nd battalion of the 36th regiment, the SS-Hauptsturmführer Günther Kaddaz. Kaddaz was remembered for his bold manner in provoking the opponent's shot across the river, having fun lighting a match in the darkness on the front line, thus unleashing the large fire of the enemy automatic weapons. Kaddaz came from the Totenkopf division, where he had been company commander and distinguished for his courage and contempt for danger. With the main effort of the Allies concentrated further east, the American troops limited themselves to cannoning the enemy lines with artillery and heavy mortars that began to shoot starting from July 17th. The Germans responded with their artillery, including the 88 mm, carefully camouflaged and the self-propelled vehicles that hid among the houses of Pisa.

The German engineers made several buildings along the Lungarno collapse with explosives to block the streets, as well as the banks of the Arno in order to facilitate the defense of Pisa. In reality Pisa had to be considered an open city or "white zone", guaranteed by the Vatican represented by the only authority recognized by the Germans in the person of the archbishop, this because of the precious monuments to be protected, as had happened in Siena which, however, , was fortunate to also host two German military hospitals: This, however, was not recognized by the Germans for Pisa who, after the capture of Rome, an open city, by the Americans, were reluctant to declare other similar areas due to the fact that the Allies had exploited the intact Roman bridges to chase the Germans with tanks, contravening the pacts. The Germans even exploited the leaning tower by installing an observatory on top which was also strafed by South African fighter-bomber aircraft. In this regard, on 25 July, Field Marshal Albert Kesserling, in command of the Italian front, ordered that no German department should approach the Leaning Tower of Pisa for at least 1.5 kilometers, which is difficult to implement, however the leaning tower was abandoned by the observers not before directing the mortar fire in the night between 23 and 24 July which forced the 1st battalion of the 91st Infantry Division to retreat south, without being able to respond to the fire for fear of hitting the monuments of Piazza dei Miracoli.

During this period the soldiers of the SS of the "Reichsführer" did not shine for their discipline, with some groups that gave themselves to the looting of houses abandoned by their inhabitants who had sought shelter from the bombings in refuges or in churches full of refugees. There are many requisitions of means and animals, as well as the appropriation of the wheat harvest, even mowed by the German soldiers themselves. There were several summary executions of civilians in the city and its surroundings, at least four episodes, mostly local Jews or young people suspected of being partisans. There was also the case of a German soldier who had kidnapped a vegetable seller who was quickly sentenced to death by a martial court for this fact.

Meanwhile, the Americans gained ground by occupying Marina di Pisa and the city airport south of the Arno in August. Subsequently, 8 kilometers east of Pisa, near the village of Zambra, on the night between 1 and 2 September, the Americans managed to cross the Arno, breaking through the weak German lines with a regiment that pointed north, to the village of San Giuliano Terme, in order to cut out German soldiers in defense of Pisa from any possible way of retreat. This forced the SS to a precipitous retreat towards Lucca and the Gothic line to escape the encirclement, leaving Pisa in the hands of the Americans, abandoned, muted, already in the night, between 1 and 2 September.

Meanwhile, on the Adriatic coast, the Gothic line withstood the impact of the Allied offensive that aimed to break through the Po valley and converge towards Vienna and the Balkans, managing to stop this advance. This was one of the last important victories of Germanic weapons on the Italian front.

Anti-guerrilla actions and reprisals on the Apennines

With the breakthrough of the Gustav line and the rapid advance of the allied armies towards the north, the actions of the partisan formations became more and more numerous. It seemed that the progress of the British Eighth Army and the American Fifth Army should end the war that summer of 1944 with the total liberation of the Italian Peninsula, which led to increased efforts against the retreating German forces, especially targeting the lines of communication and the connections of the Germanic subsistence wards. Many of the partisan attacks were conducted along the Apennine ridge and in support of the Allies along the Gothic, launching raids from the rear, so much so that the commander of the tenth army, von Vietinghoff, had to recognize the danger and combat efficiency in the eastern sector of the Gothic, where they entered the action behind the German fighters engaged against the Allies.

Along the Apennine roads and passes the partisan tactic involved the attack against the logistics and subsistence convoys, and then disappeared in their mountain refuges, avoiding direct confrontation with the more organized German soldiers.

This guerrilla was a source of strong concern for the Germanic commands who were running out of troops to be able to control the essential road arteries to bring supplies to the troops, who also found themselves with the communication routes continuously attacked by enemy fighter-bombers who did nothing but worsening a difficult situation. To remedy the partisan guerrilla, the German command, decided to implement a terrorist strategy of reprisals also against the civilian population that was suspected of collusion with the partisans or, simply, residing in the areas of partisan action and abandoned to themselves after the hit and run guerrilla operations had ended. The implementation of merciless reprisals against the civilian population succeeded in obtaining a limitation of the indiscriminate attacks against the German soldiers, given that the partisan units, rooted in a territory, hardly wanted to endanger their community, on which they also depended for the survival.

In this struggle against the partisans, some departments of the "Reichsführer" became sadly known for their ruthlessness and cruelty. In August, the SS, had to face the partisan threat in the Carrara area against the so-called "Red Star" communist brigade that threatened the front line on the Arno from the north. On August 12, to secure the mountainous territory north of Viareggio, the 2nd battalion of the 35th SS regiment was sent, at that time under the command of the SS-Hauptsturmführer Anton Galler, who, with the help of the 36th Brigade Black stationed in Lucca, they raked the village of Sant'Anna di Stazzema, gathering the population in small groups that were systematically mowed by machine guns or locked up in confined spaces where they were hit by the hand grenade launch.

The village itself was set on fire and the cattle raided or killed. The dead were 560 including 130 children. The town of San Terenzo Monti suffered the same fate, several kilometers further north, in a valley that branches off from Sarzana. Here was the SS-Panzer-Aufklärungs-Abteilung 16, led by Reder, who killed 159 civilians with machine guns between 17 and 19 August. Always Reder will be responsible for the massacre of nearby Vinca, a few days later, between 24 and 27 August. Here, too, the village will be set on fire, killing 162 civilians.

The worst massacre committed by German soldiers in Italy during the war will take place in Marzabotto between 29 September and 5 October, much further east of the Garfagnana. Here a partisan unit operated around Monte Sole and threatened the main retreat route to

Bologna of the German forces engaged south against the Americans of the fifth army, for this reason Reder and his battalion were ordered to make scorched earth against the possible bases in the mountains of the partisan guerrilla, along the road that branched from Rioveggio to Sasso Marconi. Also in this case the partisans refused to battle against the Germans, who systematically exterminated the population around Monte Sole, killing 770 civilians of which only a small part was involved in the partisan movement. This happened while the SS division was transferred to Bologna, passing under the first paratroopers corps (I° Fallschirm-Korps), with which it took part in the defense of the area of Porretta, on the Apennines.

Reder, who survived the war, was extradited to Italy in 1948 and sentenced to life in 1951 for these massacres, however escaping from captivity in 1985, to die free in 1991 in his native Austria.

Operations on the Senio embankment

During the retreat along the Tyrrhenian front, the 16th SS Panzergrenadier Division had suffered significant losses: between July 1st and September 30th the division had lost 4152 men, especially in the fighting between Cecina and Rosignano, while, between October 1st and on the 25th of the same month, there were another 1508 casualties, including deaths, injuries, prisoners and missing persons, for a total of 5660 men lost at the hands of the Allies and partisans, since the division was dependent on the fourteenth army. With the hints from Germany, the SS division brought its staff back to 14,223 men in December 1944.

Also in September, the recruited battalion that was in training in Arnhem, the Netherlands, was involved in the tough battle that took place in that town against the British paratroopers engaged in the "Market Garden" operation which saw the Germans defeat the allied forces in the their attempt to liberate Holland and occupy German soil as early as the autumn of 1944. On 24 October, the commander of the Max Simon division was replaced by the SS-Oberführer (colonel brigadier) Otto Baum, officer of the Totenkopfdivision where he had already distinguished himself in the bag of Demjansk in 1942, succeeding, in the difficult attempt, to keep the vital supply route for the salvation of the bag. Baum then reached the rank of SS-Brigadeführer (Brigadier) to the commander of the 17th division of the SS Gotz von Berlichingen before moving on to the 16th SS division "Reichsführer", at the age of only 33, with which he ended the war, also becoming one of the youngest and most decorated senior officers of the SS.

Between 5 and 26 November the Fallschirm-Korps, together with the 16th SS division, was transferred to the tenth army of Vietinghoff, engaged in the defense of the eastern sector of Gothic architecture.

The Allied offensive had run aground along the Apennine ridge but, on the Adriatic coast, a slow advance had allowed to occupy Ravenna in the first days of December, thanks to the efforts of the Canadian forces, allowing the Allies to reach close to the Po valley. To prevent the Allies from spreading northwards were the Comacchio valleys and a system of waterways and canals that made the territory difficult to armored vehicles.

The need to defend that delicate area from a trusted department fell on the SS division "Reichsführer" which was transferred there in November, in order to defend the northern embankment of the Senio river between Alfonsine and Lugo di Romagna. In December the division was strengthened by a new artillery battalion, the 3rd Abteilung, increasing the battalions of the SS-Artillerie-Regiment 16 to four, while, in January, the SS-Sturmgeschütz Abteilung was transferred to Germany to help form the 32nd SS-Freiwilligen-Grenadier-Division "30 Januar", assuming the numbering of the 32nd SS-Panzerabwehr-Abteilung in April 1945.

Between late autumn of 1944 and the beginning of winter military operations slowed down, the Allies exhausted from previous battles had to reorganize themselves to resume the offensive in the spring. Along the Senio the war became of position, similar to what was already experienced by the SS in the low and humid trenches of Anzio. Also on this occasion, the actions were limited to clashes between patrols and artillery shots, to which was added the well-known ability of the Germans to make each farmhouse and stable in a casemate bristling with machine guns.

With the opposing trenches, often a few meters away, a curious fact happened: on January 23, 1945 when, some Canadian soldiers of the 1st Infantry-Division, threw a stone with a message on a rolled sheet in the German trench, on which they asked the soldiers of the 9th company of the 3rd battalion belonging to the 36th SS regiment about the function of the hospital of Fusignano, if, there was German soldiers inside, committed to exploit as a observation point the tower placed on the structure that dominated the flat plain. The SS responded by sending a delegation composed of SS-Unterscharführer (sergeant) Willi Horne of the 11th company to parliament, under the protection of the white flag, who proposed to the Canadians to send some observers to the hospital to make sure how the structure cared for reality only Italian civilians and as there were no German soldiers inside, so there was no need to bomb the large building on which a large red cross was headed. Horne was held hostage by the Canadians who sent two officers to the German lines, who, blindfolded and taken to the hospital of Fusignano with a *schwimmwagen*[2], were able to convince themselves of the absence of enemy soldiers inside the hospital before being brought back to their lines. This fact saved the hospital from imminent destruction, saving hundreds of innocent civilians from the bombing.

If there was a relative calm on the Italian front, at the beginning of 1945, the situation was becoming critical on all other fronts. For this reason, the presence of the 16th SS division became superfluous on the Gothic line, being called back to Germany to participate in the last desperate offensives against the Soviets.

---

2 Amphibious car

▲ Soldiers of the 16th "Reichsführer" of a machine gun squad armed with an MG 42 on the Gothic front. The unit belongs to the 3rd battalion of the 36th regiment, in which the SS-Unterscharführer (Sergeant) Rudolph Michel served. The area is the one of the heights of Monterumici, just south of Bologna, where the SS definitively blocked the attack of the 34th American division between 4 and 5 October 1944, defining the front line between the towns of Vado, Monte Sole and Sant'Ansano in the Savena Valley. Note the classic camouflage used by the SS. (Alessandro Botré Collection)

▼ Back of the postcard with the caption of the place where the previous photo was taken. Note the divisional symbol of the "Reichsführer". (Alessandro Botré Collection)

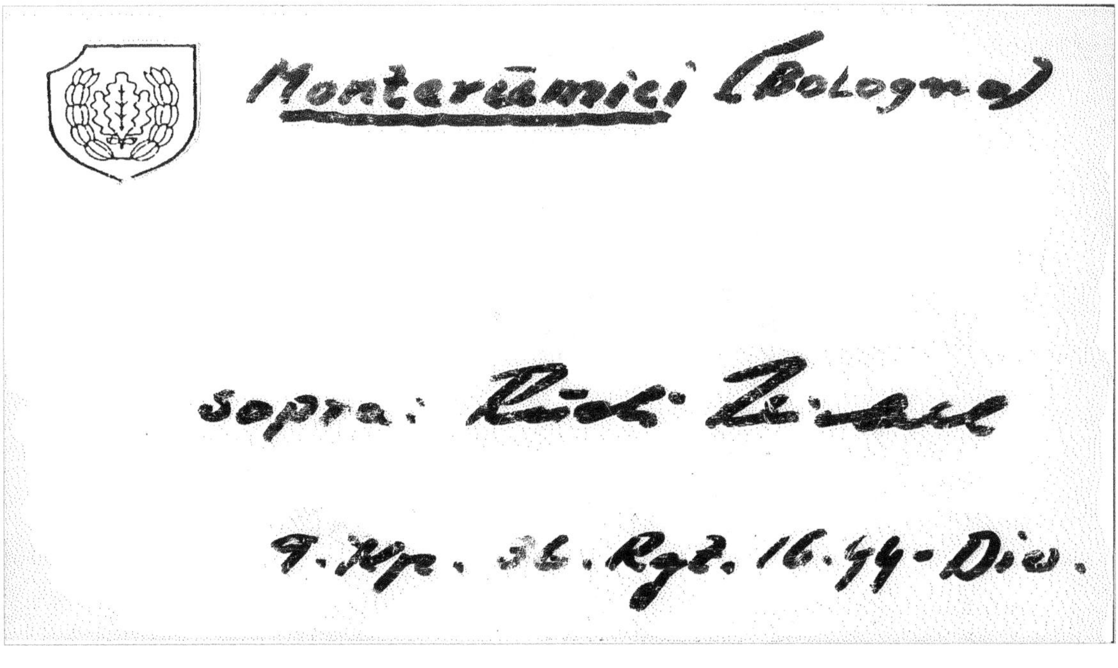

▲ Portrait of Rudolph Michel, belonging to the 9th Company of the 36th Regiment. In 1945 he was 21 years old when he was wounded on the Senio front. Previously, on that front, he was the protagonist of the rescue of an Italian boy seriously wounded in the foot by a Canadian grenade. Michel and his machine-gun squad were stationed in the nearby barn, immediately trying to rescue the boy who was transported to the military hospital in Argenta. Michel will survive the war. (Alessandro Botré Collection)

◄ Unterscharführer Rudolph Michel had made friends on the Senio line with the 15-year-old Stelio Tagle, a marò of the Decima Mas, of Wolf Battalion. At that time, the maròs had no food, so much so that they had to arrange with what they found on the spot to feed themselves, Michel shared his tin of meat with Stelio, sharing the portions with the dagger. It also happened that, one evening, they caught a chicken that ended up boiled in a helmet. (Alessandro Botré Collection)

The last offensive in Hungary

The division was transferred to Hungary in February 1945 to take part in the German offensive "Frühlingserwachen" (ie "Spring Awakening") which was supposed to lead to the reconquest of Budapest in the following month, snatching it from the Russians. This action was essential to allow the Germans to safeguard the last remaining oil wells in the region in their possession, indispensable for the war effort.
Initially, the "Reichsführer" division gathered in the rear of the Nagykanizsa oil field area, the last area with the oil resources available for the Reich.
At the beginning of March two SS army corps were formed with the main SS divisions fully booked, including the 3rd SS division Totenkopf, the 5th SS division "Wiking", the first SS division "Leiberstandarte", the 2nd SS division "Das Reich", the 12th SS "Hitlerjugend", the 9th SS division "Hohenstaufen" and the "Reichsführer". These divisions under the orders of the SS-Oberst-Gruppenführer (army general) Sepp Dietrich, together constituted the sixth armored army of the SS, the greatest concentration of SS ever occurred in the whole war, even if all these units were now under staff, weakened by months of continuous use in battle.
For this offensive, an attempt was made to exploit the surprise factor, eliminating any sign of recognition of the divisions, even the wrist straps.
The offensive started at midnight on March 5 with the Russians far from being surprised by the enemy attack, given that, thanks to the aerial reconnaissance, they had identified a strong mass of troops. The offensive developed from the north and south corner of Lake Balaton in a spring climate that had led to a rise in temperatures, starting the thaw in a region full of swamps that the melting of the ice transformed into an impenetrable quagmire, which prevented the vehicles from moving freely, especially the heavy armored vehicles had enormous problems, so much so that from Dietrich's tales we talk about 15 modern and powerful Konigstiger tanks that sank into the mud up to the turret. The artillery unleashed, that first night of the offensive, a violent barrage on Russian lines, but the German armored grenadiers, prevented from marching by the mud, could reach their attack line only at dawn and without the armored vehicles stuck in the quagmire. At five in the morning on March 6 with a new attack the SS conquered the enemy trenches.
The battle raged for three days between the mud and against an enemy superior in number and means that maintained the dominion of the skies. Dietrich's SS approached Budapest only 30 kilometers before their offensive thrust ran out due to lack of supplies, forcing the sixth SS armored army on the defensive. In mid-March the 16th SS division began the retreat by fighting along the Mur River. The SS army managed to escape the encirclement by retreating north of Lake Balaton to Austria.
Between March and April the division still had a force of about 13,000 men on paper, although in reality the valid soldiers had to be much less at that time of the war. At the end of April the remains of the "Reichsführer" division were included in the staff of the first cavalry corps (I ° Kavallerie-Korps) subjected to the second armored army that had the task of defending the region of Styria in Austria and the northern Balkans, entering in combat along the Drava River. In early May the division was divided into various Kampfgruppe who fought between Graz and Klagenfurt. On 8 May the capitulation of Germany saw the units of the 16th SS division "Reichsführer" surrender to the British and American armed forces, ending the existence of the division itself.

Organization charts

Divisionskommandeure (Division Commander)

SS-Obersturmbannführer Karl Gesele from February 1942 to September 1943
SS-Gruppenführer Max Simon from 3 October 1943 to 24 October 1944
SS-Oberführer Otto Baum from 24 October 1944 to 8 May 1945
Chiefs of Staff

SS-Obersturmbannführer Albert Ekkehard (20 October 1943 - 1 December 1944)
SS-Obersturmbannführer Karl Gesele (1 December 1944 - 5 January 1945)
Major Lothar Wolf (5 January 1945 -? May 1945)

Operations area
Yugoslavia (October 1943 - February 1944)
Italy and Hungary (February 1944 - May 1944)
Germany (May 1944 - June 1944)
Italy (June 1944 - December 1944)
Hungary and Austria (December 1944 - May 1945)

▲ 16th SS Panzergrenadier Division Reichsführer SS divisional sign

▲ Sturmgeschütz III assault cannon column of the 16th SS-Freiwilligen-Panzergrenadier-Division "Reichsführer SS"

▼ Vehicle Steyr Raupenschlepper Ost RSO-01 of the German division.

▲ Group of soldiers and NCOs of the 16th Waffen SS

▲ A couple of German paratroopers in Abruzzo in 1943

▲ Sturmgeschutz StuG-3 of the Reichsführer-SS

▼ Machine gunners in action of the 16.SS-Pz.Gr.Div. 'Reichsführer-SS

▲ Group photo of several Reichsführer-SS officers

▼ Men in tropical clothing of the 16th SS Panzergrenadier Division Reichsführer-SS

▲ Division soldiers committed in Fosdinovo, Marciaso - August 3, 1944

▲ The massacre of St. Anne was one of the worst crimes against humanity committed by German soldiers of the 16 SS Panzergrenadier Division "Reichsfuhrer SS" in Italy. In the photo is General Simon, the main person responsible for the affair.

▲ A stormgeschutz StuG-3 of the "Reichsführer-SS" being repared.

▲ A Schwimmwagen amphibious vehicle

▼ Typical recognition plate of an SS of the 16th SS-Panzergrenadier

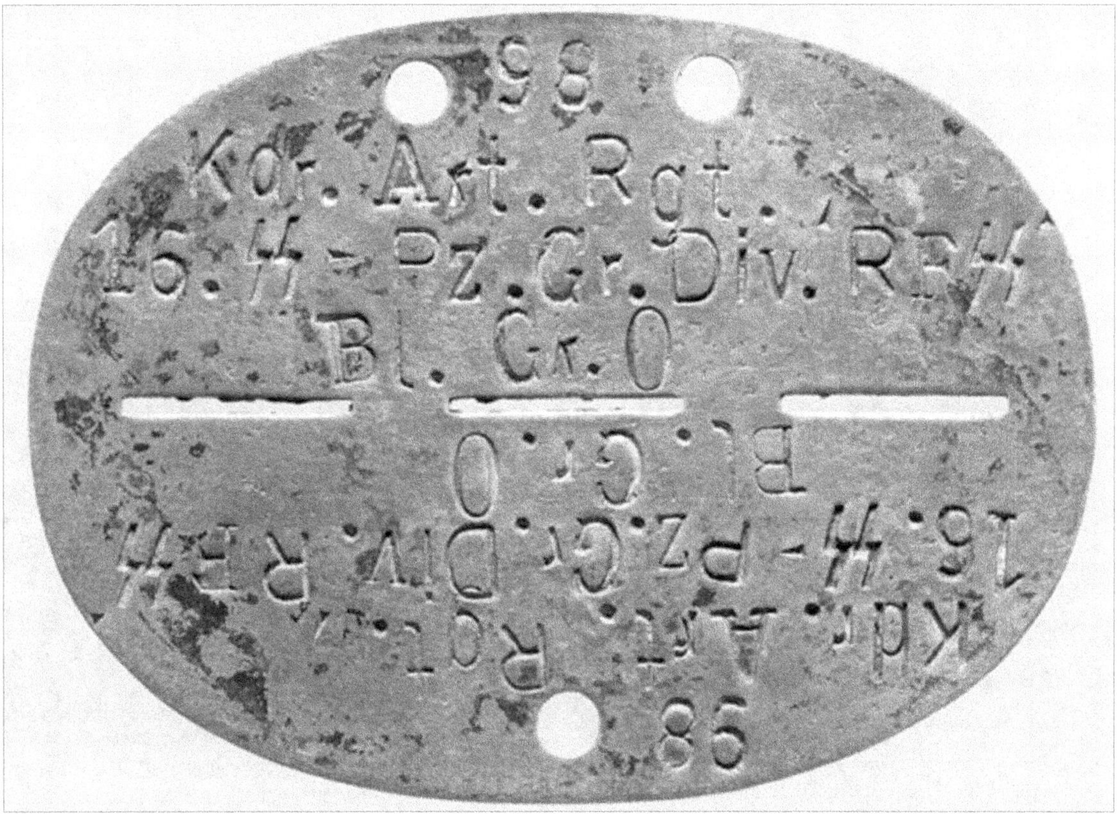

▲ Max Simon, the first commander of the division, was the main exponent of many crimes against humanity in Italy, known among them the Eccidio di Sant'Anna di Stazzema, where 560 people died, including 130 children.

▲ Portrait of Otto Baum, last division commander.

▲ Another portrait of General Baum

▲ Fallschirmjäger biker on the Italian front.

▲ Wehrmacht soldiers under the orders of the general Otto Baum

▼ General Otto Baum and Hermann Priess committed to the campaign.

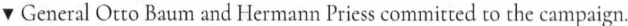

THE 24ᵀᴴ WAFFEN-GEBIRGS-DIVISION DER SS "KARSTJÄGER"

Origins

It was July 1942 when, the geologist and SS-Sturmbannführer (major) Hans Brand, proposed to Himmler to create a unit of soldiers specialized in combat in the high mountains that was inspired by the Austrian mountain troops of the previous war: the famous Kaiserjäger, and precisely the territory of recruitment would have been the same as their predecessors, between the mountains and valleys of Slovenia and Italy, the whole Central European area. The idea of a department specialized in the fighting between the gorges and the karst caves had already been hypothesized by the Ahnenerbe[3] in the 1930s, an environment present not only in Carnia but also in France, Greece, Russia and in the Balkans.

In that summer of '42 the SS-Karstwehr-Kompanie was created, a department of the SS of small dimensions but which had to be well trained in the Alpine War. Initially, an SS company from the Dachau concentration camp was deployed to Pottestein in Bavaria to be trained in mountain warfare. On November 15, 1942 the staff was expanded to that of a battalion, becoming the SS-Karstwehr-Bataillon with 3 companies of Gebirgsjäger, that is, of Alpine, since they already had reaching the strength of 1831 men in June 1942.

These mountain soldiers were called Karstjäger, the "Karst hunters". Like all German Alpine departments, the SS also used the typical Edelweiss patch (the edelweiss), sewn on the right sleeve and on the typical Bergmütze M43 cap, associated with the peculiar camouflage jacket of the Waffen SS departments. Subsequently, in August 1943, the department was transferred to the Friuli Venezia-Giulia area, the area of operation of the Adriatic Coast and the Prealps, bordering Italy with Slovenia and Croatia. After 8 September 1943, this area had been denominated as Operations zone Adriatisches Küstenland (OZAK), which saw the Slavic and Italian ethnicities confront each other for hegemony in regions inhabited by mixed populations.

With the disintegration of the Italian army, the Slavic communist faction had appropriated numerous Italian armaments, drawing a renewed vigor that was repressed only by the decisive German intervention that blocked the ethnic cleaning following the dissolution of the Italian armed forces of garrison in that area. The Yugoslav partisan formations became a real army with a widespread military organization which, at the end of 1943, allowed them to challenge the German military garrisons in the open field, the latter increasingly in difficulty on all fronts and with less and less resources to be used to control the mountainous territory of the Balkans.

To deal with this threat, the German command favored the development of local military departments, loyal to the Reich, with soldiers recruited in the Balkan area, who knew the places of employment like their enemies. In this perspective, the formation of the SS-Karstwehr-Bataillon, the Karst battalion (Karst stood for Karst), proceeded from the place where it would operate and recruit its own personnel. Already in August 1943 it was planned to recruit a new mountain division of the SS from a core of Austrian soldiers and Central

---

3 Forschungsgemeinschaft Deutsches Ahnenerbe: literally "Ancestral Heritage Research Society", aimed at researching the anthropological and cultural history of the Aryan race.

European Volksdeutsche of all ages, to which were added numerous Italian volunteers from the Karst plateaus and, more generally, from Venezia Giulia; Croats and Bosnians also joined the battalion, the nucleus of the future 24th division of the SS. Immediately after the disintegration of the Italian army, about 300 Italian soldiers joined the battalion. In December 1943 the organization chart of the Karstwehr Bataillon with the company commanders was as follows:

Stab Kompanie (command company), SS-Sturmbannführer Erich Wieland Ib
1 Kompanie, SS-Hauptsturmführer Mehrwald
2 Kompanie, SS-Sturmbannführer Kuhpantner
3 Kompanie, SS-Sturmbannführer Berschneider
4 Kompanie, SS-Untersturmführer Kühbandner
Nachschub Kompanie (supply company), SS-Untersturmführer Flake
Ersatz kompanie (company complements) based in Dachau.

In August 1943 the SS battalion settled in Val Canale, distributing its companies between the towns of Malborghetto, Valbruna, Ugovizza, and Camporosso where the battalion command was located at the "Alla Posta" hotel. Their task was to control the fundamental connection area of Tarvisio between Italy and Germany. In command of the battalion was the SS-Standartenführer (colonel) Dr. Hans Brand who had followed its development since 1942, remaining at the helm until February 1944, when, following disagreements with the OZAK command, he was replaced by SS-Sturmbannführer Josef Berschneider[4], an assignment that was made official only in August 1944. With the formation of the division, Berschneider, would gain command of the 59th Waffen-Gebirgsjäger-Regiment, which he would maintain until the end of the war.

▲ Mountain cannon 65/17 of Italian manufacture. Although dating back to the Great War it was still used by Alpine troops for its versatility and simple operation.

---

4 Born in 1902, he had previously been commander of the 5th Company of the SS-Infanterie-Regiment 6 of the 6th SS-Gebirgs-Division "North", before moving to the SS-Karstwehr-Bataillon.

▲ The mountain cannon used in action during the fight against the partisans by the SS-Karstwehr battalion. The caliber of the cannon was 65 mm.

▼ Divided into 5 parts, the 65/17 mountain cannon could be transported on the back of a mule.

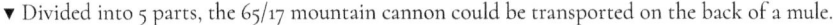

▲ Transport of the optical part of the mountain piece.

▼ The 65/17 mountain piece could also be transported when towed, as in this case, making it faster ready for action.

Antiband operations on the Carso

After the quick disarmament of Italian soldiers in the OZAK area, between September 1943 and August of the following year, the SS battalion was involved in the defense of the Treviso and Slovenian territory in a series of operations against the Communists partisan forces of Marshal Tito, very active in that border area.

The battalion's first assignment was to guard important areas for the economy, such as the railway section between Tarvisio, Gemona and Udine, as well as mountain passes and hydroelectric power plants.

Immediately after the surrender of Italy, the SS, tried to make agreements with the local partisans of the IX Korpus, freeing 56 political prisoners from the prison in Udine in exchange for the promise that the guerrillas would abandon the upper Soča valley, what that never happened, thus putting an end to any further attempt at engaging with the partisan forces. It will be the upper Soča valley that will be interested in the first counter-guerrilla operation of the Karstwehr with the aim of freeing its communication routes. The steps were blocked and the village of Saga was freed, but it was necessary to wait until October to launch an attack on the upper Soča valley and rake it from the enemy presence, this with the help of Croatian soldiers of the 2nd Kroatische Freiwilligen Legion who had heavy weapons with an artillery group supporting two battalions of Croatian infantry.

The SS and the Croatian battalions were part of the Kampfgruppe called "Bredeförder", from the name of its commander, also made up of other departments of the Wehrmacht. At that time the Karstjäger were classified in the 2nd SS Panzer-Korps led by the SS-Obergruppenführer Paul Hausser.

The operations lasted until November, still leaving time for SS soldiers to continue their training and surveillance tasks that they would share with the Croats and the 162nd (Turkistan) Infanterie-Division, infantry division (Turkmenistan), made up of soldiers of Caucasian origin, who arrived in Friuli in October. In the same period, a heavy company was formed, the 4th schwere Kompanie, with Italian war material, stationed in Malborghetto.

Always in October, the first company was busy checking the many entrenched works of the Great War, making sure that the old bunkers were not manned by partisans. On this occasion there were several skirmishes but, the most serious event, occurred on October 10, when an isolated truck of the company fell into an ambush on the road between the towns of Predil and Bretto di Sopra, which cost the Germans three deaths and 8 wounded, an episode that was soon avenged by the retaliation of the SS-Hauptsturmführer Mehrwald who, on 12 October, had 16 partisans shot prisoners and set the village of Bretto di Sopra on fire after having driven out the inhabitants. Mehrwald acted on his own initiative, coming into conflict with Dr. Brand who thought it more useful to act in moderation towards the civilians whose consent he wished and, therefore, support for the occupying troops.

Between 16 and 28 October, the 1st company with the support of a platoon of the fourth, was involved in remote clashes in the area between the inhabited area of Saga and Caporetto, with the partisans who only fired on the SS from positions on the hills and in the woods, very far from their objectives, with very little damage.

▲ Targeting the mountain cannon.

▲ The mountainous environment where the "Karst Hunters" had to operate.

▼ Ski training

Between November and December the Karstjägers were used in Operation "Treufe" which goal was to free the valleys of the Natisone and the Isonzo, between Caporetto and Cividale, from the presence of the forces loyal to Tito, through thick mounts between the fields and the wooded peaks of the region, at the same time overseeing the strategic points of passage. Several columns of the SS and the Wehrmacht, supported by heavy weapons, had as their goal Caporetto, a location reached on October 31 by the 1st and 2nd company, supported by an Italian cannon, towed by a tractor, of war prey, now belonging to the 4th ° company. The clashes were particularly hard on the heights around Caporetto where the numerous bunkers and trenches of the past war favored the defenders, forcing the SS to conquer the enemy fortifications one after the other in close encounters, between the ravines and the gullies of those mountains, often arriving in close encounters, also melee. On the night between 31 and 1 November, 800 Titian soldiers launched a counterattack to regain lost ground. The attack was repelled thanks to the shrewd use of the only heavy cannon.

Subsequently, the 2nd company led by the SS-Untersturmführer Kühbandner managed to take the comunists who had retired to their headquarters in Idresca by surprise, after they had withdrawn from the area of Caporetto, forcing the partisans to flee even from that area. . In a few days all the villages of those valleys were freed from the partisan threat.

The 1st company found itself fighting on November in the village of Stanovischis in the Natisone valley, where the comunists guerrillas fortified themselves inside a building that was conquered only after a close hard fight.

In the days of 3 and 4 November, the 3rd company, found itself cleaning the bunkers towards the Zacraio pass, where the Titini resisted strenuous resistance before being overwhelmed with 36 fallen, allowing the SS to occupy the slopes of Monte Nero, eliminating a hundred partisans.

The snow had already reached those altitudes, slowing down military operations, which continued with the raking of Monte Cucco by the 1st company and, on day 10, the 2nd company was involved in clashes in the village of Montemaggiore, south west of Caporetto, where a heavy machine gun titina, which blocked the entrance to the country, was eliminated by the personal action of the SS-Oberscharführer Alfred Ludl. Subsequently, a series of house-to-house battles developed which cost the lives of the majority of the defenders who left only 15 prisoners in the hands of the Germans. Ludl, for this and other actions, was promoted and decorated with the second and first class Iron Cross, obtaining, at the end of the war, the rare and distinctive area for the anti-partisan war, the gold Bandekampfazbzeichen[5]. This coveted decoration demonstrated the commitment against the guerrillas and the Karstjägers were the unit that had the greatest number of soldiers to obtain this recognition, so much so that the first soldier to receive it was the SS-Obersturmführer Erich Kühbandner belonging to the 24th Division of the SS.

In December the Karstjägers participated in the "Blumendraht" operation with raids between Gorizia and Trieste. During the winter, the Karstjägers were employed in a series of mopping up operations against the IX Partisan Corps of Tito around the Gradisca area. Since the

---

[5] The badge for the repression of partisan guerrilla warfare was established on January 30, 1944 and issued in three versions: Bronze, for 20 days of combat. Silver, for 50 days of combat. Gold, for 100 days of combat.

surrender of the Italians in September, Yugoslav forces loyal to Tito, had gained control of vast areas of the territory previously occupied by Italian soldiers, accumulating many abandoned weapons and equipment. Only the prompt intervention of the decisive German military formations succeeded in snatching from the partisans the positions they had easily conquered with the Italian defeat, forcing, again, the partisans, to disperse and find refuge in the mountains to continue the guerrilla war against the Germans. During a snowy day in February a small group of 15 young Karstjäger recruits from the 2nd, 3rd and 4th company on patrol at the Selva di Tarnova, ended up in an ambush being captured. Nobody knew anything until a few days later, an anonymous letter in command of the battalion, advised the SS on the place where to find their comrades, all killed and beheaded, the heads had been skewered with bayonets stuck in the ground. The fallen were buried in the cemetery of Fogliano with the date of February 19, 1944. Other sources postpone the fact to the period of the Annemarie operation, in early summer, but, probably, there must have been an overlapping of events. At that time it was normal for the partisan prisoners to be tortured and maimed and the bodies left to admonish. In response, the Germans burned the villages, deporting their inhabitants and suspected partisans were hanged.

In February the Ratte operation took place in Slovenia, between the localities of Komen and Rihemberk, during which the 3rd company, with about 250 men, ended up in an ambush hatched by the 18th titan brigade (about 900 well-equipped soldiers on three battalions) at the village of Crai / Kraj where the Karstjägers barricaded themselves on February 19, being surrounded by them. The Titines attacked the village around 1pm on that day, with the SS refusing to surrender and fighting to the last blow in a series of house-to-house actions that saw the defenders split between them inside the burning village. For the SS, the clash turned into a course with heavy losses. The relief requested via radio, were too far and failed to arrive in time to save the now compromised situation. The 4th company attacked the 19th partisan brigade the same day but was repelled by an enemy counterattack suffering the loss of three soldiers. At the same time, however, the 1st company always attacked the 19th brigade giving rise to one of the most violent battles fought against the partisans by the Karstjäger which led to the annihilation of the enemy brigade which had to complain about the death of 50 men and over 30 missing against the three fallen of the Karstjäger of the 1st company. Many of the German fallen soldiers of these battles were buried in the great shrine of Redipuglia.
With spring, military actions between Istria and the Karst, aimed at eradicating the partisan presence in the mountains, intensified. In March, several operations took place, some lasting only one day of activity, overall these were: Zypresse, Märzveilchen, Maulwurf and Hellblau, all in the mountainous area of Gorizia. This activity did not work except that of withdrawing the titin forces in remote and more inaccessible areas, towards the Tarnova forest, in addition to the capture of two American pilots shot down in the Trieste skies. On March 25, the Dachstein operation took place, in which a column of 300 Karstwehr Alpine troops led by Berschneider who from Predmeia had to reach the village of Zolla. During the mopping up there were some clashes that led to the killing of 27 partisans and the capture of 3 others, a school official was also discovered inside an inn in the town of Dol-Ottelza, immediately set on fire.

▲ Marching in column in the karstic landscape with mules packed with ammunition and equipment.

▼ Swimming pool located in the Pottenstein barracks, built in the rock of the mountain.

▲ Services room at the Karstwehr-Bataillon training camp in Pottenstein.

▼ Drilling work with a jackhammer of the limestone of the Karst for the construction of fortifications by the company of genius.

▲ The view of Pottenstein.

▲ Transporting the excavated rock material outwards.

▼ P 40 wagon employed by the Karst Hunters.

In early April, a new operation called Osterglocke developed this time in Istria, where on April 11 the 2nd company, destroyed a partisan group killing 14 enemies. By the end of the operations, the Istrian peninsula had been freed from the partisan threat. Another important anti-gang operation was called Braunschweig, in the Istrian hinterland which will lead to the capture of about 1800 partisans and the killing of another 390 with the loss, by the Germans and their Italian allies, of 35 men, including 11 killed in clashes. At the end of May the battalion was employed in the Gorizia area in the Liane operation, which began in the worst way when a convoy of German and Italian trucks ended up in an ambush that caused several losses at the village of Peternel on the morning of 22 May. That same afternoon, near that village, some Karstjägers clashed with some partisans who immediately barricaded themselves inside an inn that was set on fire together with the defenders, by the Karstjägers themselves.

On 28 and 29 May (Operation Spitz), the 2nd and 4th Karstjäger company, supported by the tanks of the 2nd company of the 208th Panzer-Abteilung, managed to free a company of the SS Prinz Eugen division that was besieged in the castle of Rifembergo by large partisan forces, the same who, two days earlier, had destroyed the 6th company of the 2nd battalion of the Tagliamento regiment. From 6 to 17 June, the Karstjäger battalion participated in the vast operation called Annemarie, carrying out a series of roundups between the villages of Buccola, Sebreglie and Idria (Idrija). On June 7, a curious episode occurred which saw three "Carso Hunters", led by the SS-Unterscharführer Süss, carry out a horse patrol in the mountains that led to the village of Recca San Giovanni, where they were supposed to join a platoon of the 15th regiment of the SS-Polizei, which soon found himself surrounded by a large partisan band. The same horse patrol was attacked by about thirty partisans near Recca. The three Karstjägers, abandoned the horses, were determined not to surrender, sheltering in a farmhouse they repelled the assailants who had come forward too boldly, killing a dozen. Besieged during the afternoon, Süss and his two companions validly defended themselves, keeping the assailants at a distance, exhausted ammunition, in the evening they managed to escape into the thick woods of the area where they hid during the day to march at night to the salvation that came after ten days of walking, when they were found by a patrol of bersaglieri of the battalion "Mussolini". All three were commended with the second-class Iron Cross.

The formation of the 24th Waffen-Gebirgs-Division SS "Karstjäger"

The need to control the territory and the successes obtained by the Karstwehr Bataillon pushed Himmler to implement the staff of the battalion which were already in significant numerical expansion, thanks to the continuous contribution of volunteers, the intent was to create a new mountain division of the SS to join the other military formations that fought in the Balkans. On July 18, 1944, with an order from the SS-FHA (SS Führungshauptamt), that means, from the headquarters of the SS, the training project for the new formation of the SS was started. On August 1, 1944, the new mountain division of the SS was officially born, which from the 3000 men of the June staff had to grow in number to become a complete division. The cadres of the Karstjägers, the "Karst Hunters", were implemented by veterans of several important SS divisions, in particular from the 6th SS-Gebirgs-Division "Nord", a mountain division of the SS. Many ethnic backgrounds among the volunteers from different countries: Ukrainians, Romanians and even Swiss, there was also a company of Spanish volunteers, most of the recruits, however, were of Slovenian, South Tyrolean and Italian origin, as well as Volksdeutsche South Tyrolean.

The structure of the division was to be the following:

SS Stab Kompanie (command company)
Waffen-Gebirgs- (Karstjäger) -Regiment der SS 59 (59th mountain regiment SS)
Waffen-Gebirgs- (Karstjäger) -Regiment der SS 60 (60th mountain regiment SS)
Waffen-Gebirgs-Artillerie-Regiment 24 (24th SS mountain artillery regiment)
SS-Panzer-kompanie (SS battleship company)
SS-Panzerjäger Bataillon 24 (24th SS anti-tank battalion)
SS-Gebirgs-Sanitäts-Kompanie 24 (24th SS health battalion)
SS-Gebirgs-Nachrichten-Kompanie 24 (24th SS broadcasting and reporting battalion)
SS-Gebirgs-Pionier-Kompanie 24 (24th battalion of the SS genius)
The two regiments of Gebirgsjäger were structured on three battalions while the artillery regiment instead had four battalions.

The new unit had unique characteristics for being a German mountain division, having equipment specially made for Karstjägers such as the Italian P 40 tanks, the best armored vehicle ever made by Italian industries. In reality the realization of this chariot was late, going back to the middle of 1943, only one tank was completed for the Italian army before the armistice. Subsequently, production continued, given the validity of the project, and the Karstjäger who benefited from it, in October 1944, were able to deploy from 20 to 22 P 40 at the armored company of the division stationed in Cividale.
Fifteen other P.40 were deployed from the 10th Polizei-Panzer-Kompanie, stationed in San Michele (Verona), and thirteen other P 40s found service in the 15th Polizei-Panzer-Kompanie located in Novara. The P 40 was an average 26-ton tank with a crew of 4 and a 75mm cannon, the range was about 150 kilometers and had a maximum armor thickness of 60mm. The P 40 was an efficient tank and could be compared, as a performance, to the German Pzkfw IV tank, even if it had the defect of not having the support of a dome for the captain.

▲ The SS-Obersturmführer Helmut Prasch, Karst fighter wearing the Gold Bandekampfazbzeichen.

▲ Helmut Prasch with his wife. The numerous decorations of the Austrian SS officer with the Bandekampfazbzeichen in gold in the foreground are evident.

▲ Close-up of the blindfolded Karstjäger officer who is taken to parliament with the British. Note the presence of the gun as well as numerous decorations including the Bandekampfazbzeichen.

▲ The same officer engaged in talks between Germans and British at the end of the war.

▲ P 40 destroyed by two English Shermans shortly before the end of hostilities, just north of Udine, near the village of Ospedaletto. The two English soldiers sitting on the hull of the German tank show the point, on a ridge, from where the English tanks fired and hit the P 40 where they are sitting.

▼ Another image of the P 40 "111" of the SS destroyed by the English tanks at Ospedaletto, the hits from the wagon are clearly visible.

▲ Karstjäger tank abandoned during the retreat in Carinthia near the Austrian village of Hermagor between 8 and 10 May 1945. Note the characteristic camouflage colouring typical of Italian armoured vehicles. The number stamped on the turret, perhaps in red, was 121.

▼ P 40 belonging to the Karstjäger (number 111) hit by enemy action and destroyed in Ospedaletto by a Sherman, along the "Pontebbana" road. You can see at least six grenade holes that hit the tank, setting it on fire and putting it out of action.

▲ British officers study the papers over the remains of a destroyed Karstjäger P 40.

▲ P 40 abandoned by the tank drivers of Polizei-Panzer-Kp.15 at the end of the war in northern Italy.

▼ Karstjäger's P 40 wagon hit by the British near Godia (Udine) and abandoned in a ditch.

In any case, the P 40 will be very usefull in the fight against the partisans who, in their memoirs, called it the "Tiger" heavy tank, mistaking it for the much more powerful German Pzkfw VI "Tiger" tank.

In addition to the tanks, were added 6 75mm mountain cannons, 4 45mm infantry cannons and 24 81mm mortars.

If the P 40 wagons were useful in the surveillance and control of the valleys, the wolf dogs were indispensable in the raids and in the identification of the partisans' hideouts. The wolf dogs were already employed inside the Karstwehr Bataillon in a small dog unit that was implemented in the formation of the division with detached teams of wolf dogs with their instructors, who came from the 4th SS Feldhundestaffel, stationed in Udine and dependent on the Hundestaffel Ost-Mitte of the Waffen SS. The dog teams operated under the Stab Kompanie of the 24th SS division which employed them in the various mopping up operations. The wolf dogs were trained for war and for the connection between departments, as well as the towing of sleds, with or without wheels, having an identification plate very similar to that of their human comrades, with the indications of the department and the freshman. One of these dogs, called Attus, was so skilled at finding the partisans' hiding places that he was given a 50,000 lire size by the partisans at the time for his capture or killing.

These peculiarities made the Karstjägers particularly fearful in the fight against the partisan guerrillas. In reality the organization chart of the division was never completed due to the scarcity of the staff available to reach the staff of a division. Only the 59th mountain regiment was formed, just as there was only one battalion of the artillery regiment, the genius battalion recruited a single company while, the panzer company, had only half of the expected staff. Due to this shortage of staff, in December 1944, the battalion was redefined as a brigade: the Karstjäger Brigade, with around 3000 actual soldiers.

The influx of new recruits, in the winter of 1945, led the Karstjägers to be renamed again as division: the 24th Waffen-Gebirgs-Division SS, when, in February, the staff reached the number of 5563 men, in perspective to complete the organization chart foreseen for the division, which will never happen.

Since the majority of the recruits came from the OZAK area, the storage and complements company, SS-Ersatz-Kompanie, was transferred from Pottenstein, where it was still based, to Gradisca and subsequently to Cividale.

In December 1944, the commander of the "Carso Hunters" was the SS-Obersturmbannführer Karl Marx who was already replaced in the same month by the SS-Sturmbannführer Werner Hahn, who remained in office until February, when with the division denomination , was in turn replaced by the SS-Oberführer Adolf Wagner who remained at the helm of the Karstjäger until the end of the hostilities.

▲ P 40 in training at Cividale, holds a demonstration in front of a group of Karstjäger lined up on the left.

▼ P 40 involved in an operation against the partisans in March 1945 at Monte Santo.

▲ Pictures with a P 40 in action during the same operation.

▼ In the foreground three platoon commanders of the heavy company of the 24th SS division, they are SS-Oberscharfuhrer Cavagna, SS-Unterscharfuhrer Dufke and SS-Unterscharfuhrer Walter, all Germans.

▲ Italian medium P 40 tank, a widely used vehicle of the 24th SS division.

▼ P 40 whose hull shows four shots from grenades that destroyed it. It's probably a wagon from a Polizei division.

The latest operations

The period of reorganization in division was carried out in the area between Malborghetto and Tolmezzo, without the Karstjäger being employed in particular operations against the partisans, even if the SS had to undergo some ambushes, such as that which occurred on 18 July against three trucks with 48 men of the 1st company bound for Tolmezzo which was attacked at the Noiaris bridge by the Italian partisans hidden on the side of the road who threw several hand grenades accompanied by the shooting of automatic weapons.
Many were wounded among the SS but, their prompt reaction, put the assailants to flight, killing two and recovering an important loot including the chest with the money of the Garibaldi Brigade. The ambush triggered a retaliation which was carried out with some cunning, with 23 SS soldiers, Italian and German, and of "Brandenburg[6]", the latter department specialized in undercover operations and infiltrations, who disguised themselves as Yugoslav partisans, who, on July 21, crossed the mountain paths south of Carinthia, killing on the spot anyone who fraternized with the fake partisans, inadvertently mistaking them for real guerrillas.
Between December and February the Karstjägers were employed to garrison the coasts of the upper Adriatic between Lignano and Cervignano, while the recruits went to complete their training and the number of staff was rising, so much so that, in April, at the end of the conflict, it was approaching to 8000 units. Between March and April, the 24th SS division participated in one last major action against the 9th Yugoslav Corps in the Tarnova forest in Slovenia.

The war was now getting to an end with the British of the Eighth Army who, in mid-April, had broken through the Gothic lines and went up to the upper Adriatic. To defend the Tarvisio pass from the Allied attack, the Kampfgruppe Harmel was formed in late April from the name of its commander, the SS-Brigadeführer Heinz Harmel, whose core was formed by the division of the Karstjäger. For the Germans there was still the idea of realizing the Alpine ridge where they could defend their metropolitan territory by exploiting the natural obstacle of the Alps. This fortified line, in the North East, exploited the old fortifications of the past world war, being called "Blau Linie "Created by the Todt organization, which was also attended by a battalion of geologists of the SS, the SS Wehrgeologen-Bataiłon 500, made up of specialists in the field. In fact, in April 1945, the fortified works were largely incomplete and devoid of defensive armaments.

With the advance of the British, the partisan formations became particularly active occupying the towns and cities, setting up checkpoints to slow the movements of the retreating Germans. On April 28 the SS 40s repulsed a partisan attack on Cividale supported by 5 Italian L 3 light tanks (possibly L 6/40), captured at the San Giusto Group a few days earlier. Last May, Cividale, was finally occupied by the Osoppo partisans, who chased the 200 SS soldiers of the garrison without fighting, while, around midday, the P 40 wagons of the Karstjäger stopped near the city cemetery. targeted by anti-tank weapons positioned in a bunker on Mount Dei Bovi, hitting several tanks that had to withdraw towards Udine leaving at least one P 40 on fire on one side of the road.

---
6 The battalion was originally a unit of the Wehrmacht, made up of volunteers, employed by the German counterintelligence and intelligence service, playing a role similar to that of the British commandos. In September 1944 the staff was expanded to the Panzergrenadier division, distorting its purpose.

Aware of the hopeless situation, the Karstjägers asked the British to continue the war against the Yugoslav communist armies to prevent them from entering Carinthia. The proposal could obviously not be accepted by the British who continued the advance towards the borders between Slovenia and Italy. It was in these areas that the only clashes that the Karstjägers had against a regular army took place. On the afternoon of May 1, at around 15.00, a retreating column of the Karstjäger armored company, with 12 P 40 tanks and several trucks loaded with SS, coming from Cividale, was stopped near Salt, just after crossing the bridge over the Torre torrent, near the village of Godia, the partisans asked for the intervention of the allied forces, who had just entered Udine. These arrived two hours later with an anti-tank platoon equipped with 6-pound pieces of which one piece managed to be put into battery. In half an hour of hard combat against the column, a tank was destroyed while the rest of the German column was able to cross the stream and continue its retreat to the north.

After the battle, while they were inspecting the P 40 hit and fallen in a pit, two British soldiers heard complaints from inside the tank; with difficulty they managed to enter the armored vehicle, where a member of the crew was still alive. This, instead of accepting the help that the two British wanted to offer him, fired his pistol and seriously injured the two British soldiers before being killed. North of Udine (near the hamlet of Ospedaletto located along the Tagliamento river) there were other clashes with the Karstjäger tank company that had no intention of giving up, despite the fact that negotiations were held. Sherman tanks climbed on a ridge line noticing some German vehicles trying to escape, supported by some P 40s. Seeing this, the British opened fire on the two P40s below them, putting them out of action.

The 24th division continued to fight, mainly against the Yugoslav partisans, trying, as far as possible, to avoid clashing with the British of the Eighth Army trying to retreat to Austria. The intent was to block the road to Carinthia from the Communists of Tito and avoid dramatic consequences for the local civilian population. The surrender of the Reich to the Allies, signed on May 7, saw the Karstjägers still armed and fighting along the passes of Lower Carinthia in an attempt to defend the Tarvisio pass against the partisans in what was considered the "Alpine Ridotto", the Alpenfestung, consisting of trenches and fixed positions in the mountains. Only on May 9, the division surrendered to the US military in Austria and the 6th British armored division that came from the south, ending the short history of this peculiar mountain division of the SS. The Karstjägers were one of the last German units to surrender their weapons in Europe.

▲ Division wristband.

▼ 24th Waffen Gebirgs-Division SS "Karstjäger" sign.

Organization charts

Names of the Karstjäger departments

SS-Karstwehr-Bataillon (1942 until August 1944)
24th Waffen-Gebirgs-Division der SS "Karstjäger" (August 1944 until December 5, 1944)
Waffen-Gebirgs- (Karstjäger) -Brigade (from December 6, 1944 until February 10, 1945)
24th Waffen-Gebirgs- (Karstjäger-) Division der SS (from 1 February 1945 until May 1945)

Divisionskommandeure (Division commander)

SS-Obersturmbannführer Karl Marx from December 1944
SS-Sturmbannführer Werner Hahn from December 1944 to February 1945
SS-Oberführer Adolf Wagner from February to May 1945

Operations area
1943
August - Tarvisio - Italy
September - November, Alto Isonzo (Soca valley) - Slovenia
November-December, Operation Treufe (Baca valley) - Slovenia
December, Operation Blumendraht (Gorizia-Trieste) - Slovenia-Italy

1944

February, Operation Ratte (Komen and Rihemberk area) - Slovenia
March, Operations Zypresse, Märzveilchen, Maulwurf, Hellblau, Dachstein, (all in the Gorizia area) - Slovenia April, Operation Osterglocke (Istria) - Slovenia - Croatia
April - May, Operation Braunschweig
May - July, Operation Liane and Annemarie (around Idrija) - Slovenia
September - December, reorganization (areas of Malborghetto and Tolmezzo) - Italy
December - February 1945, defense of coastal areas (areas of Lignano and Cervignano) - Italy

1945

March - April, offensive against the IX Corps (Tarnova forest) - Slovenia
April - May, border clashes between Italy, Slovenia and Austria

Conclusions

The 16th SS Panzergrenadierdivision "Reichsführer-SS" was part of those minor divisions of the Waffen SS (SS fighters) who helped consolidate the black legend of the SS in general which for the "Reichsführer" materialized precisely because of the many reprisals of which , soldiers, were responsible for the Apennines during the Italian campaign.
In the two short years of existence, the division was involved in only two important war

actions: the retreat in Tuscany between June and July 1944 and the spring offensive of 1945. It will be especially in Tuscany that the SS will demonstrate that they are all height of a very difficult situation, managing to contain the overwhelming opposing forces without turning the retreat en route, this with the majority of the soldiers without a real combat experience, apart from an important core of veteran officers and non-commissioned officers of many battles on all fronts.

The commitment of the division and the value of its men can perhaps be judged on the basis of the awards obtained. A single soldier of the "Reichsführer" division obtained the coveted decoration of the Ritterkreuz, the Knight's Cross1, an important parameter for assessing the fighting value of the German units. The "Hitlerjugend" division, formed in 1944, obtained 15 Knight's Crosses thanks to its participation in the Normandy campaign, while the 17th SS Panzergrenadierdivision "Götz von Berlichingen", also mobilized in 1944 and which was used in Normandy, it had only four of its components decorated as a Knight's Cross. Other important awards to the division were the 8 German gold crosses. The "Reichsführer" was engaged on secondary fronts, often with reduced staffing and materials which prevented the unit from gaining greater recognition during its short existence. Despite this, the politicized soldiers of the division had the opportunity to stand out for their fanaticism and loyalty to the National Socialist cause, obtaining the fame of the most ruthless soldiers of the whole Italian countryside.

The Karstjägers were, surely, the most successful units of the German army in the fight against the partisan guerrillas carried out in a mountain area that lent itself well to the actions of a war waged, made up of ambushes and coups by small and fierce bands. The Karstjägers also confronted in the open field with the formations of Tito's army, especially between 1943 and 1944, after the Yugoslav partisans had sacked the Italian arms depots, structuring themselves into a well-organized and numerous army that knew how to move in the territory; despite this, the German soldiers of the Wehrmacht and the SS, even if in numerical inferiority, managed to defeat them and regain possession of the territory, forcing the partisans to return to guerrilla actions between the valleys and mountains of Slovenia and Venezia Giulia, always opposed by continuous operations and roundups.

The value of the division is well indicated by the number of Bandekampfazbzeichen distributed to the division which was unequaled among all the German fighting units. The Bandekampfazbzeichen in gold conferred to soldiers of the 24th SS division were 10, 8 those in silver and 4 in bronze, against, for example, the 8 Bandekampfazbzeichen in bronze conferred to soldiers of the SS-Pol. - Rgt. "Schlanders", unit used in the same area of the Karstjäger, occupying the second place in obtaining this recognition in the German army. The Karstjägers proved to be the best anti-guerrilla unit of the Second World War, whose operating methods became an important model for future armies engaged in the war.

Hierarchy and degrees of SS

Mannschaften	Rank
SS-Bewerber	military pupil
SS-Anwärter	official student
SS-Mann	simple soldier
SS-Grenadierschüze	simple soldier 2nd class
SS-Oberschüze	simple soldier 1st class Corporal
SS-Sturmann	Corporal
SS-Rottenführer	Major Corporal
Unterführer	NCOs SS-Sergeant
Unterscharführer	Sergeant
SS-Scharführer	Sergeant major
SS-Oberscharführer	Marshal
SS-Hauptscharführer	Marshal major 2nd class
SS-Sturmscharführer	Marshal 1st class
Untere Führer	Lower officers
SS-Untersturmführer	Lieutenant (Minor)
SS-Obersturmführer	Lieutenant
SS-Hauptsturmführer	Captain
Mittlere Führer	Senior officers
SS-Sturmbannführer	Major
SS-Obersturmbannführer	Lieutenant colonel
Höhere Führer	General officers
SS-Standartenführer	Colonel
SS-Oberführer	Colonel Brigadier
SS-Brigadeführer	Brigadier general
SS-Gruppenführer	General of division
SS-Obergruppenführer	Army general
SS-Oberst-Gruppenführer	Army general
Reichführer-SS	Commander-in-chief

▲ Karstjäger engaged in fighting against the partisans.

▼ Karstjäger climbs a rock face.

▲ Climbing a path during an exercise.

▲ Karst cavities

▲ Karstic ravine. Inside you can see an SS soldier.

▲ Photo of a mountain department of the SS in Alpine training in the Alps.

▲ Karstjäger singing while marching

▼ The SS-Freiwilligen-Karstwehr Battalion training barracks in Pottenstein, Bavaria

▲ Postcard celebrating SS-Karstwehr-Bataillons training barracks in Pottenstein

▼▶ Barracks-huts in Pottenstein

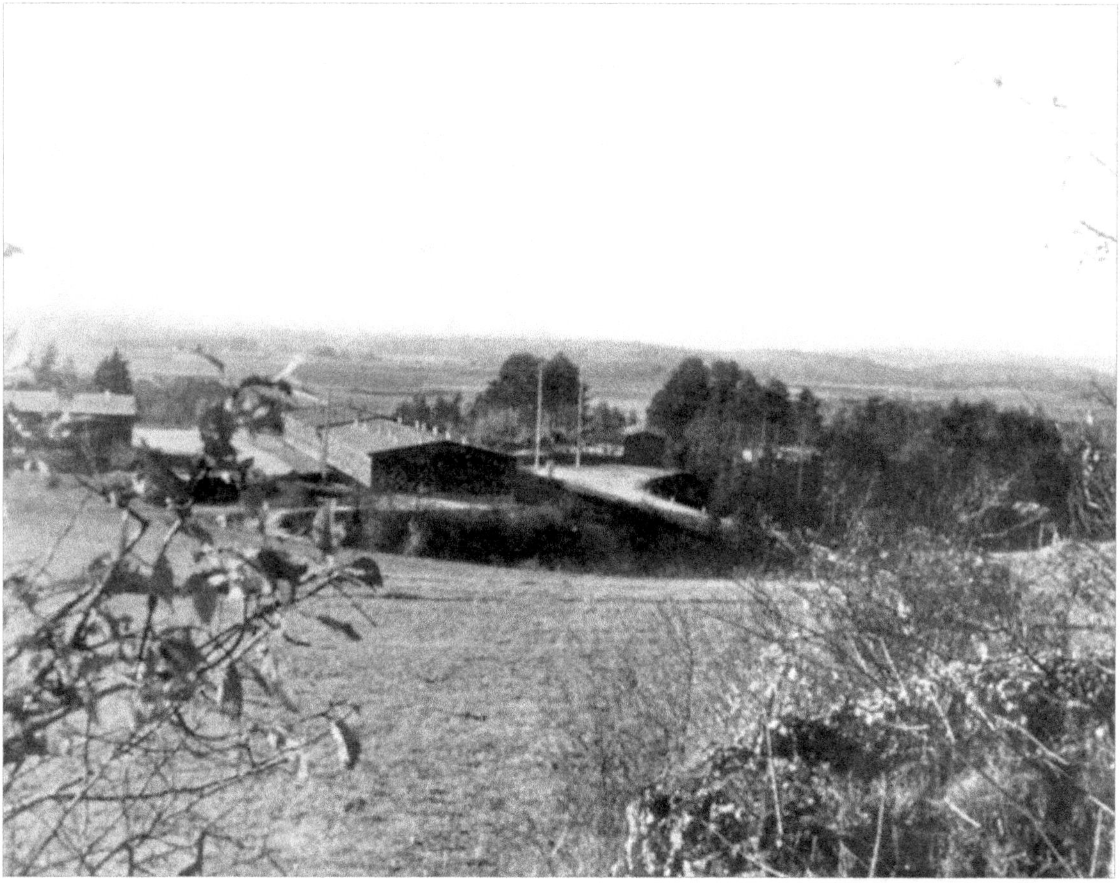

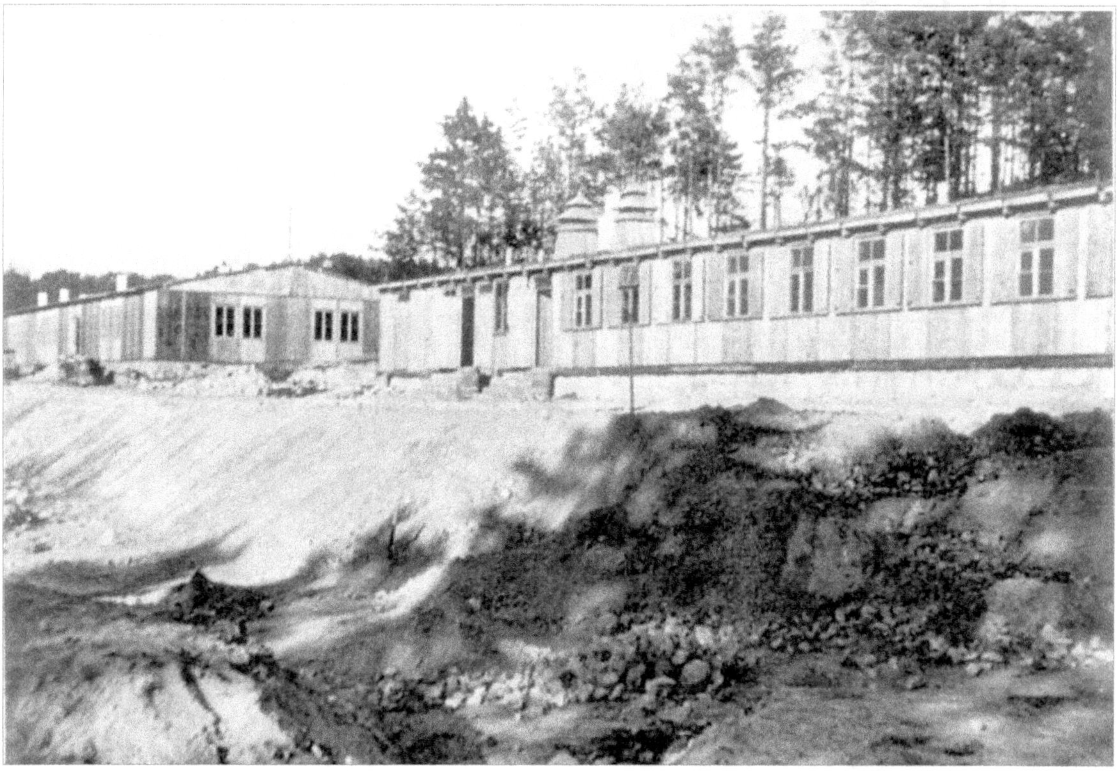

▲ Waffen-SS officer in camouflage

▼ March in the Jager Mountains

▲ Division officers group

▼ Soldiers in the barracks of Slovenia SS Foreign Volunteers and Conscripts

▲ Karstjäger on patrol

▲ Karstjäger on patrol

▲ Adolf Wagner third division commander while reviewing some of his troops

▼ Wehrmacht alpine troops training in Tirolo with the SS division.

▲ The Pz.Kp. of the 24th. Waffen-Gebirgs (Karstjäger)-Division der SS had its headquarters at the barracks "Principe Umberto" (or barracks "Principe di Piemonte"), beyond the Ponte Nuovo on the Natisone in Cividale.

▼ Men of the 9th Waffen Gebirgsjäger Regiment, one of the departments of the 24th SS Mountain

▲ Elements of the Waffen-SS "Karstjäger" Division behead a Slavic partisan in Idrijske Krnice on 11 June 1944 with brutal criminality.

▼ Surrender of soldiers and officers of the 24th to the British

▲ Karstjäger collar

▼ Engraved plate belonging to SS-Sturmbannführer Werner Hahn former division commander from December 1944 to February 1945

BIBLIOGRAPHY AND INSIGHTS

- G. Williamson, *Storia illustrata delle SS*, Newton e Compton editori
- G. Gigli, *La seconda guerra mondiale*, Lucio Pugliese editore
- F. Duprat, *Le campagne militari delle Waffen SS*, Ritter editore
- Gorge H. Stein, *Hitlers Elite Guard at war, 1939-45*, Paperback
- Robin Lumsden, *La vera storia delle SS*, Newton e Compton editori
- Sergio Corbatti, Marco Nava, *Sentire Pensare Volere: Storia Della Legione SS Italiana*, Ritter, Milano, 2001.
- Gordon Williamson, *The Waffen SS (3) 11 – 23 divisions*, Osprey Publisching, 2004.
- Gordon Williamson, *The Waffen SS (4) 24 – 38 divisions*, Osprey Publisching, 2004.
- M. Afiero, Waffen SS in guerra, *Volume IV: Battaglie e campagne dimenticate*, Associazione Culturale Ritterkreuz, 2012.
- G. Barsotti, *Pisa sulla linea del fuoco: luglio-agosto 1944*, Ritterkreuz numero 45/46, 2016.
- S. Corbatti, *La Reichsführer SS sul fiume Senio*, Ritterkreuz numero 5, 2009.
- A. Peruffo, *I soldati della divisione testa di morto*, Soldiershop edizioni, Bergamo, 2016.
- Sergio Corbatti, Marco Nava, *Karstjäger!*, Heimdal, 2010
- Sergio Corbatti, Marco Nava, *Karstjager! Guerriglia e Controgueriglia nell'OZAK 1943/45*, Associazione MADM, 2005.
- N.Pignato "*P40*", Albertelli-Storia Militare Parma 2009.
- Luca Valente, *I geologi di Himmler. L'SS-Wehrgeologen-Bataillon 500 tra Veneto e Trentino*, Cierre Edizioni, 2008.

TITOLI GIÀ PUBBLICATI
TITLES ALREADY PUBLISHING

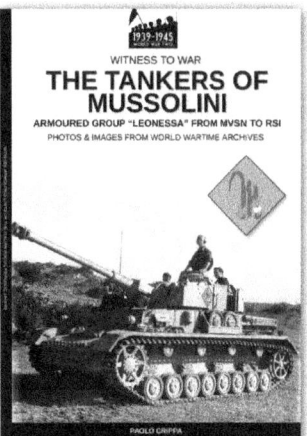
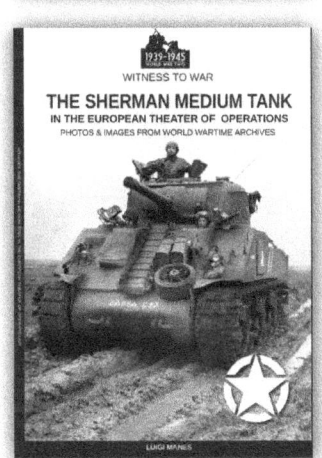

BOOKS TO COLLECT

www.ingramcontent.com/pod-product-compliance
Lightning Source LLC
LaVergne TN
LVHW081544070526
838199LV00057B/3771